MORE THAN PETTICOATS

REMARKABLE GEORGIA WOMEN

Sara Hines Martin

TWODOT®

GUILFORD, CONNECTICUT
HELENA, MONTANA

AN IMPRINT OF THE GLOBE PEQUOT PRESS

A · TWODOT ®· BOOK

Copyright © 2003 Morris Book Publishing, LLC

TwoDot is a registered trademark of Morris Book Publishing, LLC.

Cover photo: Bartow History Center, Centersville, Georgia

Library of Congress Cataloging-in-Publication Data

Martin, Sara Hines, 1933-
      More than petticoats: remarkable Georgia women/Sara Hines Martin.
         p. cm.—(More than petticoats series)
      Includes bibliographical references and index.
         1. Women—Georgia—Biography. 2. Women—Georgia—History. 3. Georgia—
      ISBN 978-0-7627-1270-0
Biography. I. Title: Remarkable Georgia women. II. Title. III. Series

CT3260.M25 2002
920. 72'09758—dc21

                                                                                    2002069758

Manufactured in the United States of America
First Edition/Fourth Printing

For my three grown daughters: Carolyn Martin,
Rebekah Martin-Fong, and Martha Martin Stevens,
who, in my opinion, are remarkable women.

CONTENTS

ℐNTRODUCTION

To borrow words from "God Bless America," Georgia ranges "from the mountains . . . to the oceans, white with foam." The remarkable women profiled in this book lived throughout that geographic range, from Martha Berry in the northwest mountains to Mary Bosomworth on the coast.

Georgia's remarkable women have come from many racial groups and have lived in various historical periods. Mary Bosomworth, who lived during the colonial period, was half Indian and half white. Ellen Craft, half black and half white, experienced the period of slavery followed by Emancipation of the mid-1800s. The African-American women in this book had to struggle against racism, and the white women struggled against the codes of their day that said that well-bred Southern women should stay at home and behave modestly.

The women here had varied amounts of education, from Mary Bosomworth, who was well educated and spoke two languages and Leila Denmark, who received a medical degree, to Ellen Craft, who could neither read nor write until she was an adult— with a wide range in between. Little is known about "Ma" Rainey's schooling, but since she started performing and traveling at age fourteen and since schools for blacks were inferior at that time, it is possible that her education stopped then or before.

These women have economic diversity as well, ranging from very poor to quite wealthy.

Several of these women were tiny physically: Mary Bosomworth, Rebecca Felton, Lillian Smith, Dr. Leila Denmark, and

Margaret Mitchell. They proved that courage, creativity, and achievement have nothing to do with physical size.

All except three of these women married. Six had no children, but most of these ladies related to and influenced children significantly, especially Juliette Gordon Low, who started the Girl Scouts, and Martha Berry, who changed the lives of mountain children at the school she founded. "Ma" Rainey adopted a son and had seven foster children, and Lillian Smith operated a girls' summer camp for twenty-six years.

These women made their marks in many different areas, illustrating their own unique talents and personalities. They persisted against odds; they dared; they were bold when the circumstances called for boldness; they broke barriers; they challenged the status quo, often in service to others rather than for personal benefit.

They excelled in a variety of fields: education, politics, music, writing, social work, art, working with youth, architecture, and medicine. It is likely that Georgia's story would be extremely different without the involvement of these women. Still, they are just a sampling of the many remarkable women who have influenced the state.

Writing this book has been a rich experience for me. As I lived with this project, I felt that I came to know each woman personally. Researching each story was like reading a mystery, wondering how things would turn out for each woman. Would she conquer her particular set of odds, and—in particular—how? Would Mary Bosomworth lay claim to her properties? Would Ellen Craft and her husband get caught in their attempt to escape from slavery? Although I knew in advance that Rebecca Felton pulled out of the post–Civil War poverty she and her husband found themselves in, I didn't know how or to what extent. How *did* Nellie Black do so much, even with household help? When would

Juliette Low move out of her life of wealth and self-indulgence to accomplish the task for which she is so well known?

How would Martha Berry raise enough money to keep her schools afloat? Would Lugenia Hope win her battles against racism in general and against the Atlanta school board in particular to get better schools for blacks? Would Leila Wilburn get a secure foothold both financially and professionally in Atlanta's male-dominated world of architecture? Would Lillian Smith ever see results from her campaign to end segregation in the South? And while researching Margaret Mitchell, I wondered: Will Scarlett get Rhett back? Except for the last, my research answered all of these questions and they will be answered for you in these pages.

MARY MUSGROVE BOSOMWORTH

CA. 1700–1765

Pocahontas of Georgia

From adolescence until the end of her life, Mary Musgrove Bosomworth, as she is remembered in history, straddled two worlds: her Indian heritage and her white way of life. She lived like the English with regard to home, clothing, marriage, and political activity, but she remained strongly connected to the Native American peoples. Both cultures respected and misunderstood her.

The circumstances that thrust Mary into the spotlight of history actually started in England in 1729. General James Oglethorpe, a soldier, statesman, and humanitarian, secured a commission from King George II to establish the Colony of Georgia in the New World. Oglethorpe hoped it would serve as a haven for Europe's oppressed, especially debtors and religious refugees. The king signed the charter for the colony that would be named for him on June 9, 1732.

In November 1732 Oglethorpe—the only member of the trustees of the colony charter to actually travel to Georgia—left England with about 120 colonists. The ship stopped in South Carolina, then Oglethorpe and a few others paddled boats up the Savannah River. He spotted a bluff that would provide a good location for a settlement.

GEORGIA HISTORICAL SOCIETY, SAVANNAH, GEORGIA

The Bosomworths Invade Savannah, from Lawton B. Evans's
First Lessons in Georgia History (1913).

The Yamacraws, a split-off group of Creek Indians, lived
about 3 miles from the bluff, so the spot was called Yamacraw
Bluff. Tomochichi, their *mico,* or chief, greeted the English.

Oglethorpe wished to ask permission for his band to settle on
the bluff, yet neither man spoke the other's language. The chief
sent for Mary Musgrove, the daughter of his sister, the old matri-
arch. The chief also had a brother, Old Brim, called "Emperor of
the Creeks," so the Indians had given Mary the title of princess.
Mary spoke English well and translated between the two leaders. In
addition she helped placate the Indians' objections to the English
settling there; and over the years she monitored transactions

between the Indians and colonists.

Oglethorpe hired Mary, agreeing to pay her one hundred English pounds—some say two hundred, while some say he promised her nothing—per year. The general treated her with "great Esteem" and made her his emissary to the Creeks.

Tiny Mary, standing five feet tall and weighing one hundred pounds, was thirty-three years old at that time. Her black hair hung in two long braids and she stuck a feather into a band of beads she wore across her forehead. One colonist wrote that she was "an Indian woman in mean and lowe circumstances, being only Cloathed with a Red Stroud Petticoat and an Osnabrig shift." Mary later disputed that report, saying that she and her husband were "on the verge of great riches."

Mary's story has roots in the settling of South Carolina. When the English settled Charlestown (later Charleston), South Carolina, in 1670, the Creek Indians welcomed them to get protection from other Indians and the Spanish friars who were establishing missions and converting Indians. Henry Woodward, responding to this welcome, established a trading center at Coweta, a major Creek town on the Ockmulgee River.

However, the Creeks' loyalty to the English did not last long. In 1715 they joined forces with their relatives—the Yemassees— to attack Charlestown, starting the devastating Yemassee War. From the Creek point of view, the attack was a failure. The Creeks then sought Cherokee help to pursue another attack, but the Cherokee aligned with the Carolinians against the Creeks. After the Creeks sought protection from the French and the Spanish, they signed a peace treaty with the Carolinians that ended the war. The Creeks and the Carolinians began to trade again in 1718.

Mary was born around 1700 in Coweta. Her Creek name has different spellings: Cousaponakeesa, Cooszaponakeesa, Coosapon-akessa, or Consaponakeeso. Although the identity of her father is not certain, John Bee, the leading Indian trader in this period, has been considered a possibility. More recent scholarship, however, proposes that Mary's father was more likely Edward Griffin, a licensed trader, or possibly Henry Woodward.

When she was between the ages of seven and ten, Mary's father took her to Pomponne—now Pon Pon—in Colleton County, South Carolina. There the girl was baptized and educated as a Christian, learned to speak English, and was given the Christian name Mary. Mary stayed there for the war's duration.

In 1716 the government of South Carolina sent Colonel John Musgrove to negotiate the treaty that would end the Yemassee War. His son, John Musgrove Jr., accompanied his father and fell in love with the Indian "princess" and asked her to marry him. The bridegroom, an Indian trader and government agent, probably had a Native American mother. Colonel Musgrove may have arranged the marriage, which took place in 1717. Although Mary married two more times, she is best known today by the name Mary Musgrove.

The newlyweds lived among the Cherokee in Georgia for several years. They then returned to South Carolina about 1723 and lived there for more than seven years. They had two sons, Edward and James. They relocated in June 1732 to Yamacraw Bluff, the site of present-day Savannah, a year before General James Oglethorpe founded the Georgia colony.

At the request of the Creek Nation and by the consent of South Carolina Governor Robert Johnson, the couple opened a trading post. Mary, an extremely talented woman, showed her skills in business, and the trading post grew significantly. One-sixth of Charlestown's annual export—twelve thousand pounds of deerskins—passed through the Musgroves' hands. They also owned cattle and three Native American slaves.

When Oglethorpe settled the new colony of Georgia, he gave Mary gifts to secure her friendship. Georgia had few leaders among its small number of early settlers and, in order to survive, those settlers had to establish relations with the local Indians and those in South Carolina. Oglethorpe often called on Mary to interpret and negotiate between his government and Indians. In one instance Mary used her influence to convince the Yamacraw Indians to cede a portion of their land to the colonists. Oglethorpe admired and trusted her so much that he began to regularly seek her advice, which did not set well with some of the other Englishmen.

Both Georgia and South Carolina vied to have the upper hand in trade with the local Native Americans and in the rum trade. Mary helped Georgia win in that rivalry when she negotiated travel agreements between the British in Georgia and the Chocktaw. In 1734 Mary again used her influence when she interpreted at the meeting between Chocktaw Chief Redshoes and Georgia's leaders.

Two years later, when tensions arose, Oglethorpe again asked Mary to serve as interpreter at a meeting with Chigilly, leader of the Lower Creeks, and Malchi—Brim's son and Mary's cousin—who would succeed Chigilly.

Two or three years after the Musgroves moved to Georgia, John Musgrove died. Different sources list his death as 1734, 1735, and 1739. At the time of his death, Mary had a home in Savannah and 1,400 acres of land. She also held an important position in the colony because of her relationship with Oglethorpe and her ability to provide supplies to the early settlers.

Mary received a condolence letter from Oglethorpe. She did not remain widowed for long; she soon married Jacob Matthews. At the time, Matthews, who came to Georgia as an indentured servant—and possibly had been Mary's servant—commanded twenty rangers stationed near the new trading post. "His marriage to Mary completely changed him," E. Merton Coulter wrote in his article, "Mary Musgrove, Queen of the Creeks: A Chapter of Early Georgia Troubles." "He was now a 'lusty . . . Fellow' . . . who became . . . 'blown up with Pride.'" Quarrelsome and given to drink, he gathered about him the colony malcontents. Coulter continued:

> A man of this disposition would not fail to make full use of the Indians and to employ all the means in his power to secure the aid of Mary . . . in his plans. He and Mary were soon complaining that the Indians were not being given their full quota of presents, and to better play on their sensibilities he frequently made them drunk. . . . During the period of her alliance with Jacob, Mary had begun to show signs of being weaned away from the best interest of the colony and the fact that she did not drift further away was, perhaps, due to the presence of Oglethorpe.

Mary's influence in the colony continued during her five-year marriage to Jacob Matthews. Oglethorpe asked Mary to start a second trading post on the south side of the forks of the Altamaha River at Mount Venture to help protect Georgia against Spanish invasion. Mary would look out for any suspicious Spanish movements and try to warn the colonists.

She aided in concluding treaties and in securing Creek warriors to fight with the British against Spain in the War of Jenkins' Ear, 1739–44. Mary influenced the Indians to side with Oglethorpe, and she even sent her own traders into battle. Creek warriors went with Oglethorpe when he attacked the fort at St. Augustine, unsuccessfully, in 1740. Mary's brother, Edward Griffin, who had acted as Georgia's emissary to the Creeks, died in the battle, along with other family members.

Around 1738 a group of Creeks gave Mary title to three offshore Georgia islands, Sapelo, Osaabaw, and St. Catherines, plus a tract of land that Oglethorpe had ceded to the Creeks in earlier treaties.

Jacob Matthews became ill in 1742 and, although Mary took him to Savannah for medical care, he died on May 8. Yamasee or Spanish Indians demolished Mary's unprotected trading post at Mount Venture, taking away her cattle and raiding the Yamacraw post.

Mary continued to barter with traders at Yamacraw. She also sold colonists meat, bread, and other foods that were sorely needed in those early years before the colonists began to produce these items themselves. Many of the colonists never paid their bills, so she virtually gave away a lot of produce, losing about 826 English pounds due to bad debts.

In 1743 Oglethorpe left Savannah, giving Mary a going-away present of one of his own diamond rings, taken from his finger, valued at two hundred pounds. To demonstrate his esteem and appreciation for her services, he promised her one hundred pounds a year to continue as interpreter and promised two thousand more pounds to sweeten the pot.

Again, Mary did not remain widowed for long. Coulter wrote, "When it came to marrying, Mary was either designing or gullible; it seemed she could have no rest unless she was married to somebody." She married Englishman Thomas Bosomworth on July 8, 1744.

When Oglethorpe left, he recommended that William Stephens be made president of the colony and consequently leader of the governing council. Thomas Bosomworth worked as a clerk for Stephens, who later appointed him as secretary of Indian affairs. He had volunteered to fight alongside Oglethorpe at St. Augustine before traveling to England to take holy orders, after which he was appointed the Church of England's minister to Georgia, serving at one time as chaplain to Oglethorpe's regiment. He later abandoned his religious calling and became an adventurer, described as a man of "sprightly Temper" with a "Little Share of classical Learning." The Bosomworths opened a new trading post on a spot called "the Forks," where the Ockmulgee and Oconee Rivers met.

Although her benefactor, Oglethorpe, was gone, Mary continued to help the colony. During the War of the Austrian Succession, she worked successfully to convince the Creeks not to respond to the French appeal for help. During the Creek-Cherokee war in 1747–48, she persuaded the Creeks to remain loyal to the English after the Spanish courted them.

Although Coulter wrote that it was during Mary's marriage to Jacob Matthews that her attitude toward the colony changed, it wasn't until after Oglethorpe left that relations between Mary and the colonists turned hostile. First, the colonists no longer treated Mary with her former respect, which insulted her. Mary also felt angry about the lack of payment for the goods and services she had provided colonists. She had continued to interpret for colonial leaders, according to her agreement with Oglethorpe, and it was when Mary asked for the payment that Oglethorpe had promised her that relations between herself and the whites became strained.

A major conflict occurred when Mary and Thomas Bosomworth attempted to lay claim to the property Mary had received earlier from the Creeks. Georgia leaders denied Mary's claim to ownership of the islands, and she would spend much of the rest of her life fighting to secure British recognition of her claim. Most historians believe that Thomas Bosomworth influenced—and misled—his wife, convincing her that the colonists had wronged her. When referring to Thomas Bosomworth, historians use words and phrases such as "foment a scheme," "take advantage both of the Creeks and of the colony government," "ambitious," "an unscrupulous fortune seeker," "adventurer," "carpet-bagger," "a troublemaker," and "fortune hunter."

In *A History of Georgia*, William Bacon Stevens took an especially cynical view of Bosomworth. He wrote:

> Hitherto the career of Mary had been one of generous self-denial, and of unmerited labors for the good of the colony. She had not indeed received the full reward of her services; but she rested in security on the faith of the government, and was, until her marriage with Bosomworth, quiet in her conduct, and moderate in her demands. But, from 1744 [the date of her marriage], her whole was changed; and the colony . . . was now, through her misdirected influence, to feel the dreadful horrors of expected massacre and extermination.

Up until 1743 Mary had received only about one thousand dollars, so she had a justified claim, but Stevens wrote, ". . . her avaricious husband . . . stepped in with an exorbitant demand for nearly twenty-five thousand dollars."

However it came about, Mary's attitude toward the colony shifted from friendly to adversarial. After the couple had been married one year, Thomas Bosomworth went to England, writing the trustees of the colony that he would not return. After he had been in England for two years, though, he came back to Georgia. For the next two years, he stirred up the colony with his attempts to get compensation for Mary's services and to get the property. In addition he gave up all ecclesiastical duties and defied the colony trustees' ban against slavery by bringing six black slaves in from South Carolina for his and Mary's use. The trustees sent the slaves back, which doubtless angered Thomas Bosomworth.

Bosomworth secured the support of Major William Horton, Oglethorpe's commander of the regiment from the town of Frederica, Georgia, and other officers. When Colonel Alexander Heron arrived in 1747 to replace Horton, he supported the Bosom-worths. Thomas gathered a group of Indians, led by Malatchee, Mary's brother, to confer with Horton. Malatchee summarized Mary's services and asked that Thomas's brother, Abraham, be sent to England to plead Mary's cause to the king. Thomas Bosom-worth proposed that the Indians crown Malatchee king, and it was done. The Indians deeded to Mary all their hunting lands "from the fourth day of the wintry moon and so long as the waters run down to the ocean forever." By 1750 Mary had secured the signatures of seven Creek Nation chieftains who supported her demands for payment of past services and her demands that certain lands be deeded to herself and Thomas.

The Creeks supported Mary in her claims and threatened to block any further colonial settlement in areas agreed upon under the Creek-Colonial treaty of 1739. The situation became so combative that Mary, presenting herself as queen of the Creeks, led about two hundred Creeks into Savannah on August 7, 1749. Thomas Bosomworth walked beside her in his canonical robes. The Indians fired guns as they walked, indicating their support of Mary, and William Stephens and the council members became understandably alarmed.

The council entertained the Indians at a banquet where rum flowed freely, and they convinced them that Bosomworth was trying to take lands that belonged to all the Indians. Mary, also intoxicated, rushed into the meeting and threatened the colonists, who arrested her and her husband.

Upon her release she continued her battle.

Abraham Bosomworth took documentation to England, hoping the king would recognize the legitimacy of Mary's property ownership. Thomas, optimistic about a positive response, bought a herd of cattle from South Carolina merchants on credit. Mary, Thomas, and the cattle settled on St. Catherines Island.

The Board of Trade in London, in turn, received strong documentation from the Georgia colony stating that Creek leaders disputed Mary's claims. Feeling that their cause could be pursued more favorably in person, Mary and Thomas sold some of their property to raise cash to pay for a trip to England.

When the couple arrived in Charlestown in 1752 to begin their trip, they were caught up in the aftermath of a Lower Creek Indian uprising. Near there, a Creek, Acorn Whistler, had killed four Cherokees and taken another prisoner. Horses had also been stolen from the Indian traders. Prior to the attack, both Indian groups had pledged friendship before the colony's governor, James Glen, and the South Carolina Council. Thus Glen, who felt that his authority had been challenged, requested that the Council appoint Mary as agent to resolve the dispute.

The Council resisted the governor's request. They agreed to Mary acting as interpreter but appointed Thomas Bosomworth as agent. Thomas would be paid seven hundred pounds for the negotiations. The Bosomworths spent five months among the Creeks and successfully negotiated terms agreeable to both sides.

Mary remained with the Creeks until the spring of 1753, and Thomas returned to Charlestown in January to take care of their fragile financial situation. Creditors in the city were hounding them, and they had exhausted their trip funds to pay for the Creek treaty mission. It was only through Governor Glen's intervention with writs of protection that the couple stayed out of jail.

The matter became more tense when the Commons House of Assembly defied Glen and dismissed the couple's requests for payment. Thomas appealed to the General Assembly and Glen for nearly a year. Relief came in May 1754 when the Commons House authorized 2,266 pounds for Thomas. The issue was not resolved, however, because the public treasurer refused to release the total amount. Thomas responded by filing a lawsuit, but he left the state before the matter came to trial.

The dispute took a new turn in June 1753 when the trustees of Georgia gave ownership of the colony over to the King of England. In 1754 the Bosomworths made their trip to England. To their disappointment the Board of Trade rendered a decision in 1759 that disallowed their claims. When they returned to Georgia, Mary accepted a compromise in 1760 from Henry Ellis, who had been recently been appointed governor of the state. William Bacon Stevens wrote, "Thus after long years of litigation, after the most threatening disturbances, after scenes of turmoil and chicanery that embroiled the colony almost in civil war, and put in serious jeopardy its best interests, was this troublous claim adjusted to the satisfaction of all parties, and up on terms honourable and beneficial to each."

The colony council and governor resolved the issue by giving Mary title to St. Catherines Island and cash from the sale of Ossabaw and Sapelo Islands. The acquisition of St. Catherines plus her earlier properties made her the largest landowner in Georgia. The Bosomworths relinquished all claims against the government in June 1760. They had enough money to build a grand home on St. Catherines, where they lived until Mary's death in 1765.

Mary Musgrove Matthews Bosomworth is buried on St. Catherines Island.

In *Unsung Heroines of the Carolina Frontier*, Alexia Jones Helsley wrote: "Mary . . . was a remarkable woman. At a time when the 'troika . . . wife, mother, and household mistress,' defined the lives of most women, she exercised extraordinary influence not only in Creek–Georgia relations but also as an emissary of South Carolina. Few women in her time approached her level of importance."

"Mary Musgrove Matthews Bosomworth rose to become an outstanding leader," wrote Linda K. Kerber in *Women of the Republic: Intellect and Ideology in Revolutionary America.* "She was a woman without equal on the Carolina–Georgia frontier and one who contributed profoundly not only to the success of the Colony of Georgia but to the success of the Carolina venture as well."

Historians hold differing viewpoints about Mary's value to Oglethorpe and thus to the colony of Georgia and her status in history. Some consider her one of the most important figures in Georgia's colonial history and an outstanding woman. Some take a more cynical view. However, she undoubtedly provided an invaluable service to Oglethorpe. Surely the development of Georgia would have gone quite differently without her aid.

SARAH FREEMAN CLARKE

1808–1896

Nineteenth-Century Artist

*S*amuel and Rebecca Clarke presented their first daughter, Sarah Anne, to Samuel's stepfather, Dr. James Freeman, a Unitarian minister, for baptism at King's Chapel in Boston on March 13, 1808. Sarah Anne, born January 21, would later change her middle name to Freeman in honor of her step-grandfather.

Sarah grew up in Dorchester, Massachusetts, with four brothers, Samuel, James, William, and Abraham. A fifth brother, Thomas, was born later. The children amused themselves by riding horses, fishing in a nearby brook, and picking blackberries. In the summers they visited Freeman's summer home, where he escaped his hectic Boston schedule.

Freeman had stature in the community as a founder of King's Chapel—the first Unitarian church in America—and served as an important father figure for the grandchildren. A colleague described him as ". . . generous in gift and deed, graceful, gracious, simple, sincere, never unmindful of the rights or feelings of those who differed." Samuel Clarke, the children's actual father, was a well-educated but restless man who bounced from vocation to vocation.

Sarah Freeman Clarke

Every summer morning Dr. Freeman assembled his grand-children outdoors for classes in Greek and Latin, supplementing these subjects with riddles in trigonometry. When rain drove them inside, they studied literature.

Sarah's maternal grandfather, William Hull, was equally distinguished, yet in quite an opposite field. He was a U.S. Army general who, when ordered to invade Canada from Detroit in the War of 1812, surrendered to the British rather than have his troops massacred. A U.S. military court accused him of treason and pronounced the sentence of hanging. Because of his remarkable service in the Revolutionary War, however, General Hull's sentence was later commuted. He returned to his farm at Newton, near Sarah's home, and during the children's daily visits there, they heard the general recount tales of his frontier military exploits.

Through her extraordinary grandparents and their contacts, Sarah met many other outstanding persons. The first was General Marquis de Lafayette, the Revolutionary War hero, who gave the Clarke children a great deal of attention. Sarah also met some of New England's best artists, which encouraged her interest in painting. When she was ten, famous portrait artist Gilbert Stuart sketched General Hull. The general introduced Sarah to the artist, boasting of her artistic ability.

In 1816, Sarah's father moved the family to Boston, where he worked as a druggist and a medical advisor. Each Sunday they sat in their reserved pew—the one nearest the pulpit—at King's Chapel. When Sarah's mind wandered during sermons, she kept herself occupied by observing the stately Corinthian columns and other features of the unique building.

When Sarah was seventeen, she went to an exhibition opening at the prestigious Boston Athenaeum by herself, shocking proper Bostonians. Sarah explained that "she could attend the exhibition unattended by a gentleman."

Shortly after this, General Hull and his wife died. Rebecca Clarke became pregnant with her sixth child, a distressing situation since Samuel's business had once again failed and the family's financial situation was troubled. Samuel and Rebecca's attempts to keep their sons in Boston Latin School and Harvard added to the financial strain. Rebecca increasingly turned to her daughter for emotional support. The baby, Thomas, was born in 1827.

George Curtis, a relative who imported cloth, asked Samuel to purchase a chemical bleaching factory. He did, and the Clarke family returned to Newton in 1829. The next year, the factory—which was uninsured—burned. Samuel died later that year at age fifty-one. At the time of his death, his debts totaled six thousand dollars and his assets totaled fifty dollars. Rebecca Clarke was now a widow with a young son, Thomas, and no financial prospects. She again turned to Sarah for comfort, and the two women sought inspiration from Washington Irving's *The Sketch Book:* "There is in every true woman's heart a spark of heavenly fire, which lies dormant in the broad daylight of prosperity; but which kindles up, and beams and flames in the dark hour of adversity."

The women soldiered on. They opened a boardinghouse called Ashburton Place. They employed a cook, a handyman, and a chambermaid. The house was in a choice location: Harvard lay only a few miles away, and Boston Common was even closer. King's Chapel, eating establishments, galleries, and lyceum lecture halls were within walking distance. The business got off to a good start—due in part to Rebecca's social skills. Sarah must have been shy in groups, because a young friend wrote: "When young Sarah Clarke ate with the group, she blushed at the slightest cause. . . . Her mother labored to keep the dinner conversation at a polite and cheerful level."

Circumstances slowed the success of the boardinghouse, however. All the staff fell ill during an influenza epidemic in 1831.

Rebecca and Sarah nursed their sick employees, did the work of the staff, and took care of the guests. Sarah observed that her mother never caved in under the distressing circumstances that beset her but frequently said, "I am almost discouraged!"

By 1833 Ashburton Place had a good reputation for hospitality. Former guests not only returned but also stayed for long periods. In the evenings visitors could attend lectures at the nearby halls or play parlor games. Sarah earned extra money by teaching art lessons.

The departures of her brothers caused Sarah sadness during this time. William and Abraham moved first to St. Louis and then to Chicago. Samuel moved to Augusta, Georgia, hoping the warmer climate would improve his rheumatic conditions. He later joined his brothers in Chicago. James, who had been studying at Harvard, could not afford to stay at the school. He first taught school nearby and then attended divinity school, visiting his mother and sister frequently to discuss what he was learning about Unitarianism. He later moved to Louisville, Kentucky, to take a position as a newspaper editor. Throughout her life family remained of preeminent value to Sarah.

Friendships were also highly valued by Sarah, and she developed enduring ones. The Peabody sisters, Mary and Elizabeth, stayed at the boardinghouse, and the three developed a strong bond. Sarah would also later meet the third sister, Sophia Peabody, who married Nathaniel Hawthorne.

Each spring Sarah took part in fund-raising fairs for charitable causes. In September 1833 Rebecca closed the boardinghouse to spend the winter with her sister and Samuel in Augusta. Sarah then returned to Newton, where she took care of the aging Dr. and Mrs. Freeman and her brother Thomas, now five.

Sarah continued to attend King's Chapel each Sunday. Dr. Freeman still served as pastor, and in this position he began to meet people involved in what was called the "The Flowering of New England." This movement—lasting from 1820 to 1850—grew out of the intellectual and artistic pursuits of historians, poets, and scholars of Boston, Cambridge, and Concord. Most of the leaders were Unitarian ministers connected by the intellectual spirit of transcendentalism, a belief that valued individualism and the goodness of the natural world. They believed that knowledge transcended the physical environment, and they committed themselves to making the world a better place.

Among the leaders of this movement were Ralph Waldo Emerson, James Freeman Clarke, Oliver Wendell Holmes, Edgar Allen Poe, Nathaniel Hawthorne, Horace Mann, and Horace Greeley. Women, especially those who were intellectual and single, moved from the fringe to the center of the movement. This number included Dorothea Lynde Dix, Elizabeth Peabody, Julia Ward Howe, and Edna Littlehale Dow Cheney.

Sarah received many of the people involved in the transcendental movement in her home, so the movement put her in touch with interesting and stimulating personalities. She met more famous people, including Oliver Wendell Holmes. Elizabeth Peabody introduced her to Louisa May Alcott's father, Bronson Alcott, who ran a school in Boston. Sarah, who had had some negative experiences with teachers at school, liked Alcott's school because he did not use the usual corporal punishment. She enrolled Thomas, who had been called a "handful," and he thrived there. Sarah and the controversial Alcott became lifelong friends. She taught drawing at the school, donating her services when he couldn't afford to pay her.

Sarah and Rebecca again experienced financial problems brought about by the approaching Bank Panic of 1837—the worst financial panic in the nineteenth century. They feared that they might have to go live with Abraham or William in the Midwest.

At the end of the 1835 school term, though, Sarah and Rebecca had enough money to go to Newton for the summer, and they took Thomas with them. Dr. Freeman died in November. Rebecca traveled to Augusta, while Sarah and Thomas stayed in Newton to take care of their step-grandmother.

Sarah kept busy painting, and that winter the Boston Athenaeum exhibited two of her paintings. On her frequent visits there, she worshipped from afar a Harvard-educated aristocrat named Washington Allston, whom many thought as talented as the outstanding Italian painter Titian. Sarah and Washington eventually met, and Sarah was delighted when he invited her to one of the private gatherings he held after his exhibitions.

In the midst of these activities, Sarah found time to help Elizabeth Peabody teach Sunday school at King's Chapel and to attend lectures. She was especially impressed with the lectures Ralph Waldo Emerson gave. Sarah found herself moving in the same social circles as Emerson.

It was time for Sarah to make a decision in regard to what she wanted to do with her life. Did she want to be an educator? Or perhaps a full-time artist? Such a vocation was virtually unknown for women at the time. Yet the transcendental movement had begun to influence art, leading people to want realistic landscapes and nature scenes rather than romantic styles. In *Sarah Freeman Clarke, 1808–1896: A Woman of the Nineteenth Century,* Joan Alice Kopp wrote:

> Few nineteenth-century women dared to approach art as a profession. Sarah Clarke was an exception. Her formal art career began slowly as she wrestled with decisions concerning her future and periods of self-doubt. She listened to James Freeman Clarke extol her literary

promise while Bronson Alcott and Horace Mann beckoned for her to fulfill the need for participants in educational reform. Preoccupied at the same time by her fascination with Emerson's lecture topics, Sarah appeared unable and unwilling to focus on a singular pursuit. Often, feelings of frustration resulted from her inability to capture the creative inspirations, which seemed to drift fleetingly in and out of her daily activities. While family still came first for Sarah, the young woman was uncertain as to which direction the intellectual part of her life should take.

James Clarke thought Sarah needed to make a decision away from her familiar surroundings and family obligations, so Sarah spent the winter of 1836 in Louisville with him, painting while there. They had long conversations about the directions Unitarianism was taking, especially about dissensions within the movement.

The time spent in Kentucky brought out Sarah's artistic vitality, which had been submerged by her responsibilities in New England. Sarah returned to Boston in the spring of 1837 by way of Chicago, where she visited William and Abraham. While there, she heard Daniel Webster speak.

After her return to Boston, she began her greatest work, *Kentucky Beech Forest*. The Boston Athenaeum exhibited that painting more than fourteen times between 1840 and 1860.

That winter, due to Elizabeth Peabody's efforts, Sarah met the reclusive Nathaniel Hawthorne. She became lifelong friends with him and his wife, Sophia Peabody. This fact alone speaks of Sarah's charm: Hawthorne had few female friends.

Sarah continued to vacillate in her decision about becoming a full-time painter, wondering if she had true talent. Elizabeth

Peabody approached Washington Allston, asking him to evaluate Sarah's paintings. When the two women went to Allston's studio in the summer of 1838, he examined her sketches and canvases carefully and said that he "regarded it as her duty to be a painter. . . . I do not hesitate to advise you to make landscape painting your profession."

Sarah rented an apartment near Allston's studio and began to take daily classes from him. All the creativity she had buried for years came forth. She wrote James several months later, "My only trouble now is that I feel in such a hurry to paint all those pictures which have been hoarded in my brain for years that I scarce can stop to attend to any one in particular."

Sarah paid ten dollars to attend weekly "Conversations" led by outspoken feminist Margaret Fuller in Elizabeth Peabody's bookstore. Sarah served as Margaret's assistant. The group, which discussed various topics such as education, Grecian mythology, and transcendentalism, impressed the members of the city's closely knit intellectual circle. Some of Boston's most cultivated, prominent, and politically active females attended the meetings, including Mrs. James Russell Lowell, Mrs. Horace Greeley, Marianne Jackson— Oliver Wendell Holmes' sister-in-law—and Julia Ward Howe.

Joan Alice Kopp wrote:

In all, over forty women participated in the famed sessions which, in some ways initiated an emancipation from the traditional nineteenth century role of women. The significance of the meetings lied [sic] partly in the importance they held for spreading liberal doctrines, as well as for propagating ideas of the feminist movement. Those attending later initiated other discussions of special interests that led to reforms in many areas. Some, such as Julia Ward Howe, assumed active roles while others, such as Sarah, remained more passive.

Margaret Fuller recognized Sarah's great intellectual and literary potential. According to the custom of the times, she would pass a collection of Sarah's letters around to others. Margaret wrote: "I send also letters of Sarah Clarke's which I think will charm you with their dignity of tone and elegance of expression. . . . And are not in the letters elegance, self-possession, accurate perceptions, a love of beauty?"

Ralph Waldo Emerson also became impressed with Sarah while she faithfully attended his lectures. Having never met her personally, he invited her to Concord and later wrote that she was "a very true person but with the right New England frost in her nature forbidding the streams to flow."

Those who attended the "Conversations" decided that the group needed to publish their viewpoints. Emerson organized a club, of which Sarah was a member, that published a magazine in which the transcendentalists could express their thoughts. The first issue of *The Dial,* published in July 1840, contained a poem by Sarah.

The transcendentalists felt so optimistic that they could achieve a perfect society that some planned to organize an ideal community. George Ripley left his post as a Unitarian minister in 1841 to found the Brook Farm Institute of Agriculture and Education near Boston. Sarah often visited the dozen families who moved there in the spring of 1842 to live communally. In 1847 a fire brought an end to the project.

Meanwhile, Sarah influenced the direction her brother James's life would take. James, unhappy with divisions within the Unitarian church, moved to Pennsylvania with his new wife. Sarah proposed that he start his own church in Boston. James made a complete break with the Unitarians and, in April 1841, Sarah and Rebecca joined forty-five others who signed the membership charter for the Church of the Disciples. James preached each Sunday in a rented hall to the group that included Dr. Samuel Cabot and Julia Ward Howe.

After Grandmother Freeman died in 1841, Sarah had the freedom to travel. Her inheritance from her grandmother and the income she received from her paintings gave her the needed finances. In the summer of 1843, Sarah, James, and Margaret Fuller spent four months visiting Samuel, William, and Abraham in Chicago.

After the travelers returned home, Margaret wrote a book called *Summer on the Lakes,* in 1843, to which Sarah contributed etchings. In the book, Margaret commented on the role of women and Indians on the frontier, yet it was Sarah's artwork that clearly displayed their plight for readers.

Sarah—along with many other Americans—developed an admiration for European culture. In 1844 she, her mother, and her brother James went to Italy to view the country's landscapes and art. Sarah became part of the colony of Americans and English who enjoyed Rome's stimulating environment. After two winters, though, Sarah succumbed to Rebecca's loneliness and the two returned home.

In the winter of 1852, Sarah persuaded Rebecca to return with her to Italy to join James and his wife there. They spent two winters in Rome, basking in the cultural atmosphere. Rebecca returned to Boston, and Sarah again traveled back to America at her mother's urgings. Sarah used her Italian experiences to produce fourteen paintings between 1856 and 1860. Rome always remained dear to her heart.

In 1860, as the war between the North and South neared, Sarah, her mother, James, Massachusetts Governor John Andrew, and two female Clarke relatives opened the Home for Aging Colored Women. The Clarkes had relatives in the South and were unable to choose sides during the war. James's church members drew their reluctant pastor into abolitionist efforts, and he bought the site of Brook Farm and turned it over to the military for training ground. He also suggested to Julia Ward Howe that she write some new words to the familiar tune "John Brown's Body." Inspired by a battle she witnessed, she wrote a poem to go with the tune, and the famous song "The Battle Hymn of the Republic" was born.

In May 1865, after becoming wealthy from her investments in Chicago real estate, Rebecca Clarke died. She left nearly everything to Sarah.

In 1868 sixty-year-old Sarah returned to her beloved Italy with her niece, Lillian. The next year Sarah—a Dante scholar—and Lillian made a pilgrimage following Dante's path in the fourteenth century. Sarah filled her sketchbooks along the way. The women then rented an apartment in Rome where Sarah hosted many guests from New England. Sarah produced a three-by-four-foot book of pen sketches based on the Dante trip that was exhibited in a New York studio.

In 1871 Sarah received news from William and Samuel that the Great Chicago Fire had burned their homes, destroying their art collections and the collection of letters Sarah had written over a forty-year period. She visited them, bringing pieces of Italian art to replace their loss.

In December 1872 Sarah and an art patron from the United States made a three-month trip down the Nile River. As usual, Sarah took her sketchbook.

In 1877 Abraham and Samuel Clarke decided to move south for health reasons, choosing Marietta, Georgia, northwest of Atlanta. Soon after Abraham and Samuel arrived, they received the news that William had died suddenly. This same message brought Sarah home from Rome in the fall of 1879. She also visited her brother Thomas, now an engineer in New York.

Rome had changed Sarah, who now signed her middle name as Freeman in honor of her grandparents. She now had greater self-confidence in contrast to her earlier reticence. A rarity in the nineteenth century, she was one of the first women to declare art as her profession.

Sarah moved to Marietta to care for her brothers. She enjoyed life there and had a large home built west of the town square. She set out to learn gardening and Southern cooking.

The longer she lived in Marietta, the more she loved the physical beauty of the area. She spent a lot of her time sketching or painting outdoors. She also lent some of the books she had collected throughout her life to her family and new friends, and from this informal beginning, a library began to take shape. She allowed people to check out her own personal books and even gave her library a name: the Franklin Lending Library, probably after Ben Franklin's Philadelphia library. When someone asked for a book Sarah didn't have, she sought help from James, who was then a trustee at the Boston Public Library.

Sarah's enthusiasm for her new project—and information that she needed $2,200 to achieve her goal of starting a real library—stirred generous feelings in her New England friends. They held a fund-raiser and sent her books. Dr. Oliver Wendell Holmes sent her copies of the twelve volumes he had written. Sarah then proposed that her library merge with the Marietta Library Association. She made two requests: that the library continue and that the association donate a lot for a building to house the books. The association granted both, raising twelve hundred dollars to buy a lot.

Sarah, wanting the new library building to be unique, proposed a design inspired by two men: Sir Anthony Panizzi, the assistant librarian of the British Museum, who had suggested that a dome-shaped addition be built, and phrenologist Orson Fowler, who liked octagonal buildings. In the summer of 1893, the brick, eight-sided, one-story, thirty-foot-high Sarah Freeman Clarke Library was constructed on the lot bought by the association on Church Street near the town square.

Sarah donated two thousand books for the library, which officially opened on October 26, 1893. The green marble plaque above the door reads:

THIS BUILDING AND MANY BOOKS
ARE A GIFT FROM FRIENDS TO THE
CLARKE LIBRARY ASSOCIATION OF MARIETTA
OCTOBER A.D., 1893

APPLY THY HEART UNTO INSTRUCTION
AND THINE EARS TO THE WORDS OF KNOWLEDGE
PROVERBS OF SOLOMON

Though her health was declining by this time, Sarah remained cheerful and mentally alert. She received guests at her Marietta home, including Julia Ward Howe.

Sarah Freeman Clarke died on November 17, 1896. She rests in the St. James Episcopal Church cemetery with her brothers Samuel and Abraham and Abraham's wife, Susan.

Volunteers staffed the library named for her until 1920. Miss Lillian Clarke of Boston sent monetary donations to the library until her death in 1928. The library opened two branches before merging into the Cobb County Library system in 1959. A new Marietta branch of the county library system opened in 1989. The original Clarke Library building still exists and is now occupied by a private business.

ELLEN CRAFT
1826–1891

Runaway Slave

"Stop them! Catch those runaway slaves!" the ticket agent called as the young white man and his male slave jumped on a train in Macon, Georgia, on the morning of December 21, 1848. At least that is what appeared to have happened.

The young white man, a Mr. Johnson—actually Ellen Craft, a fair-skinned slave—and her "male slave"—actually her husband, William Craft—were beginning their escape to freedom. The ingenuity with which these slaves, illiterate and with little money, developed and carried out this plan was remarkable. The trip, possibly the most dramatic escape from slavery ever recorded, would take them 4,000 miles.

Ellen dressed as a well-to-do white man with his right hand in a sling, supposedly due to rheumatism. Because Ellen could neither read nor write, use of the sling would ensure that she would not have to sign hotel registers. She also wore a bandage on her cheek, a scarf wrapped under her chin and over her cheeks as if she had a bad toothache, and green eyeglasses shading her eyes. These disguises served to prevent her from being recognized as a female,

Artist's rendition of Ellen Craft during her flight to freedom.

especially because they covered her smooth face. Along the way, she would pretend to be deaf to avoid talking to fellow travelers.

Ellen and William boarded the train just moments before its departure. As they took their seats, they narrowly escaped detection. In fact, William's employer was running the length of the train, peering into windows, looking for the runaways.

The groundwork for their plight had been laid decades before, when a group of Englishmen established the colony of Georgia in 1733. At that time, Georgia had the distinction of being the only colony that banned the owning of slaves. After several years, however, many people concluded that the only way they could develop the economy would be to use slave labor. Therefore, by 1750, the rewritten charter permitted slaves. In December 1829 the state legislature made it a crime to teach slaves to read or write. By 1860 Georgia had nearly as many slaves as white citizens. Ellen and William were two of the many victims of the cruel system.

Ellen's master, Major James Smith, one of Macon's founders, was also Ellen's father. According to the custom of the day, a white slave owner could father children by a slave woman. Ellen was born in 1826 to Maria, one of Major Smith's many slaves. The law regarded Ellen as a slave like her mother rather than free like her father. The child resembled her father more than her mother, however, especially in having his fair skin.

Ellen's mother worked in the owner's house, so Ellen was raised in better circumstances than most other slaves. She lived in comfort, for example, rather than in a dirt-floor cabin as other slaves did. House servants had plenty to eat, in contrast to field hands who might eat only once a day. The work that house servants did was also lighter than the work done by field hands. Instead of chopping cotton in the hot sun and getting calluses on her hands, Ellen performed duties such as dusting furniture and setting and clearing the table. She also learned useful skills, such as sewing, at which she excelled.

Owners could beat their slaves any time they chose, and the presence of her husband's child by another woman enraged Major Smith's wife. Ellen's mistress slapped her, scolded her, and boxed her ears, and Ellen was helpless to protect herself against the constant abuses. Ellen's father treated her like any other slave; he did nothing to protect her from his wife's actions.

Even though Ellen's situation could have been much worse than it was, she complained often to her mother. Her mother tried to help her daughter by saying, "But you are so much better off as compared to the field slaves. The most important thing is that you cannot not be sold away from me." Owners could—and often did—sell children away from their parents and siblings away from siblings, but Ellen's father protected Ellen from that fate. He had forbidden the sale of his own child.

Eventually, Mrs. Smith found a way to get the constant reminder of her husband's infidelity out of her sight. She gave Ellen to her daughter, Eliza, when she married. Thus, in 1837, Ellen became the slave of Dr. and Mrs. Robert Collins. Although this event removed her from a dreadful situation and placed her in another enviable setting for a slave, the move also took her away from her mother.

Robert Collins, a wealthy bank owner, had 10,000 acres of farmland and sixty-two slaves. Although Ellen's new mistress treated her well, Ellen continued to be unhappy because she knew she could now be sold or given away as if she were a piece of property. She grieved for the plight of other slaves and vowed never to marry and have children who would be slaves like her.

Unbeknownst to Ellen, the young man who would cause her to break her vow was living not far away. William Craft's life, however, had been quite different from that of the woman who would one day become his wife. His parents, also slaves, had been married, unlike many slave parents who were not, and they had five children. The family had a stable, loving home life and worked very hard for their master. Because of their loyalty and the fact that their master's vast land holdings and cotton fields required the labor of many slaves, the family felt secure from ever being sold or separated.

They were wrong, however. As was common at the time, their master eventually sold William's parents when they grew older and could not work as hard. To add to that cruelty, the owner sold William's parents to two different buyers, and they never saw each other again. The children comforted each other in their sorrow, but they were soon faced with a new sorrow. The owner sold one brother and one sister, each to a different owner.

William must have wondered if he too would be sold. His master had him apprenticed to a cabinetmaker and his brother to a blacksmith. Slave owners earned money by hiring out such trained slaves to other people. These slaves could keep some of the money earned from their trades; thus William built up a store of money.

Soon, however, his owner's financial problems affected William's comfortable life. William's brother was sold, and later, when William's owner could not pay a bank loan on time, the bank took ownership of William and his sister. The two young people found themselves on the slave auction block so the bank could recoup its money.

William's sister was the first of the pair of siblings to go through the humiliating process of the auction. First she was examined as if she were livestock, then she was bid upon and finally sold. As William mounted the block, he pled first with his sister's new owner to wait and then with the auctioneer to delay his work so he could say goodbye to her. Neither man agreed. William's last glimpse of his sister was the sight of her riding away in a cart, crying.

Ira Taylor, who worked at the bank owned by Ellen's new master, bought William. William worked at his trade of cabinet-making and at a nearby hotel as a waiter, saving the money that aided his future escape. He met Ellen several years later; the two fell in love, but they resisted marriage, remembering the pain of being separated from their parents. Over time, though, their owners granted them permission to live together as husband and wife on the Collins's property. The couple pledged never to bring into the world children who would become slaves. And they began to dream and talk of escape from slavery.

Ellen and William faced seemingly insurmountable obstacles to secure freedom. They knew what could await them if their escape attempt failed. Usually men on horseback tracked slaves with bloodhounds, and the slaves were horribly beaten after they were retrieved. Ellen could pass for white because of her skin color and the manner of her speech, learned while living in her master's house, but the law required a slave to have a written pass from his or her owner to travel by stagecoach, boat, or train. Even if Ellen could get away, however, William probably could not. Neither wanted to leave without the other.

William came up with an ingenious plan: They would travel by train to the North. Since a white woman would not travel alone with a male slave, Ellen would pose as a white male and William would pose as her slave. At first, Ellen thought the plan would be impossible, but her desire for freedom overcame her fears. She told William, "God is on our side; with His assistance, we will be able to succeed."

It fell to William to buy the items for their disguises. This was a difficult task because state law forbade slaves from making purchases at shops without their masters' permission. Some stores, however, sold directly to slaves so they could make more money. William went to different shops to buy their clothes, except for

Ellen's pants, which she, with her sewing skills, made herself.

The couple needed only one other item: written passes for their travel. Ellen asked her mistress if she could visit a dying relative some distance away, and William asked his employer for permission to accompany his wife. Both received the coveted passes, which they could not read. This reminded them that Ellen could not write and thus would not be able to sign her name on a hotel register. It then occurred to her to pretend to have an injured hand.

Eight days after conceiving the plan, the couple was ready to leave their cabin. William cut his wife's hair short. The two, both deeply religious, knelt in prayer, asking God's help for their journey. As they stood, William whispered, "Come, my dearest, come. My love, our first step toward freedom." Ellen, who would remain remarkably calm during the entire journey, at that moment was overcome with fear. She fell onto William's chest, sobbing silently. She then regained her composure, and they stepped into the night.

But the cabinetmaker to whom William was apprenticed suddenly had second thoughts about giving William permission to leave and rushed to the train station to intercept the couple. Ellen and William barely escaped capture.

William, posing as Ellen's servant, had to sit in the last car, the customary place for slaves to ride. Ellen met her first challenge when she took her seat on the train. The man seated next to her, a frequent guest at the Collins's home, had been a dinner guest there the night before! When he attempted a conversation, Ellen pretended to be deaf. By listening to her fellow passengers, Ellen learned for the first time that abolitionists, who had been spoken of with derision by whites, actually helped slaves gain freedom.

The train took Ellen and William to Savannah, where they transferred to a steamer headed to Charleston, South Carolina. The ship had no place for Negroes to sleep, either slave or free, so William slept on the deck. At breakfast the next morning, fellow passengers warned "Mr. Johnson" (really Ellen) about taking his slave north, predicting that the slave would run away. One man even offered to buy William right then.

That night, Ellen and William stayed in one of Charleston's best hotels. As they were leaving the next day, Ellen encountered another challenge. She asked the chief customs officer to sign "Mr. Johnson's" name for him, but he refused to do so. A fellow passenger from the steamer intervened, and the captain signed the name.

Ellen and William boarded a new steamer bound for Wilmington, North Carolina. From Wilmington, they took a train for Richmond, Virginia. Because of Ellen's "invalid" condition, she was seated in an apartment with a couch at the end of one car. She shared the space with a Southern gentleman and his two daughters. What happened during that trip actually made Ellen smile. Learning of "Mr. Johnson's" rheumatism, the gentleman wrote out a cure, saying he had the same illness. The three even urged "Mr. Johnson" to lie down, making a pillow out of the women's shawls and covering Ellen with the man's coat. Thinking "Mr. Johnson" was asleep, one young woman confessed to her sister that she felt attracted to the young man! When they left the train, the gentleman gave Ellen his card, inviting him to visit their home in the future.

As they were nearing Richmond, Ellen and William had another scary moment. A white woman mistook William for her runaway slave and demanded that he come with her. Ellen feared that she might need to show her ownership papers, but the woman realized that she had made a mistake.

The couple got off the train at Fredricksburg, Virginia, and took a steamer for Washington, D.C. From there they took a train to Baltimore, the last port in slave-holding territory that they stopped at, arriving on Christmas Eve, 1848.

When they boarded the train to Philadelphia, they encountered another crisis. A Yankee officer demanded that "Mr. Johnson" provide proof of ownership of his slave. Because other passengers expressed sympathy for the ill "Mr. Johnson" and because the conductor of the train from Baltimore vouched for the trustworthiness of the pair, the officer let them go.

But the crises had not come to an end. The exhausted William fell asleep near the baggage car. When the train reached Havre-de-Grace, Maryland, the passengers got off and took a ferry across the river before boarding the train again on the other side. William slept through the entire procedure, and Ellen panicked when she could not find him. Ellen feared that William had been captured. They were reunited, however, on the far side of the river.

Their next stop was Philadelphia. It was Christmas Day. They found lodging at a boardinghouse. Ellen burst into tears, saying, "Thank God, William, we are safe!" The couple believed that they were free. Ellen took off her disguise.

In Philadelphia Ellen and William learned about the Underground Railroad. They also met their first abolitionists, one of whom was a free Negro named William Still. Although the Crafts had planned to go to Canada, their new friends advised them to go to Boston. Although U.S. law would not shield them from being captured and sent back to Georgia, Boston's strong abolitionists protected runaways.

A Quaker farm family living outside of Philadelphia gave the Crafts shelter for three weeks, but Ellen found it hard to trust whites. The family proved themselves trustworthy, however, and the children taught the runaways to read and write. After the three weeks, the couple moved on to Boston, where they met Frederick Douglass, an ex-slave and abolitionist leader, and the Reverend Theodore Parker, a minister. These two were part of a group who befriended and protected the Crafts.

William found work in Boston as a cabinetmaker and Ellen

as a seamstress. The couple soon started speaking at abolitionists' meetings with William Wells Brown, a fellow runaway slave. Brown sometimes charged a fee, which was an unusual practice and offers some insight about the quality of the speeches the Crafts made and the sympathy the public felt for them.

The speaking engagements placed them in jeopardy, however. A Macon, Georgia, newspaper reprinted a notice that had been placed in a Boston newspaper to advertise one of these events. Robert Collins and Ira Taylor had by then learned where their runaways had gone. Knowing how difficult it was to get a slave out of Boston, however, the owners took no immediate action.

A year later, in 1850, President Millard Fillmore signed into law the Fugitive Slave Bill under which anyone who helped a runaway slave could be fined one thousand dollars and could spend six months in jail. If a runaway were arrested, he could not speak in his own defense in court. The judge could decide whether or not the person were slave or free; if declared a slave, a U.S. Marshall could, with the help of the army if needed, return him to his master.

Reverend Parker formed a Vigilance Committee in the Boston area to help protect slaves from capture. Many slaves fled to Canada, but the Crafts remained in Boston. Shortly after the passage of the law, a man from Macon, Georgia, came into William's place of work and tried to convince him and Ellen to meet him at night. Luckily, the Vigilance Committee learned in time that the man was a slavecatcher whom Collins and Taylor had hired to return the Crafts to them. The committee found a safe home where the Crafts could hide.

Fearing that they would be captured and returned to their owners, the Crafts decided to leave the United States. At first they planned to sail from Boston to England, but ships on that route were being searched for runaways. Their second plan was to slip away to Portland, Maine, and from there to board a ship for England.

William and Ellen wanted to have a legal wedding ceremony before leaving Boston, so Reverend Parker married them on November 7, 1850, prefacing the ceremony with these words to William: ". . . If a man attacks you, intending to return you to slavery, you have a right . . . to resist the man unto death; yet you might refuse to exercise that right for *yourself.* . . . But your wife is dependent upon you. It is your duty to protect her. . . . I charge you, therefore . . . to defend the life . . . of your wife, against any slave hunter."

Reverend Parker then wrote a letter to President Fillmore, pleading with him to change the Fugitive Slave Bill. Parker did not receive an answer to his letter. About the same time, Collins wrote a letter to the president, protesting the fact that his slave (and her husband) had not been returned from Boston. The acting secretary of state answered the letter for the president, reassuring Collins that he had ordered U.S. troops to be sent to Boston to arrest William and Ellen.

Despite the risks, the Crafts pursued their dream of freedom. More obstacles, however, impeded their goal. Reverend Samuel May, Jr., another member of the Vigilance Committee, accompanied the couple on the trip to Maine by train. The three could not relax until they reached Portland because law officers often rode on the train looking for runaway slaves. Having passed that hurdle, they learned that their ship had been damaged in an accident hours before, preventing it from sailing.

An abolitionist kept them in his home for a time, but William and Ellen decided to take a ship to Canada and then go on to Liverpool. Before they left, Reverend May gave them a letter to take to his friend Dr. Estlin when they reached Bristol, England.

The couple went on to St. John's, New Brunswick, where they encountered hurdles similar to those they had met farther south. The hotel manager agreed to give Ellen lodging but refused

William because of his color. From St. John's, they took a steamer to Windsor, Nova Scotia, two days later. Then they travelled by coach to Halifax, an expensive and tedious overland route. Once in Halifax, they planned to board a ship bound for England. On the coach, William had to ride with the driver in the rain. Both he and Ellen caught bad colds. A broken wheel then delayed the coach's arrival, and the ship left two hours before the Crafts arrived in Halifax. They learned that the next ship to England would not leave for two weeks.

Again they had problems getting lodging because of William's color. A black minister and his wife kept the couple. The steamship line refused to sell them tickets, claiming that the steamer was full, but through the intervention of an influential abolitionist, William and Ellen got their tickets.

On the ship, Ellen's cold turned into pneumonia. One night, she and William held hands and prayed because William feared she would not live through the night. She survived, and the two reached Liverpool two years after their departure from the South. "It was not until we stepped upon the shore at Liverpool that we were free from every slavish fear," William wrote. They knelt and kissed the soil.

Happy years followed. A minister kept the Crafts in his home for a short time; then Dr. Estlin took them to his Bristol home. William and Ellen again linked up with William Wells Brown, who had also fled to England and had become an ardent speaker against slavery. The Crafts themselves spoke out on the subject and led a demonstration against American slavery at the Great Exhibition of 1851 at the Crystal Palace in London.

They began their own formal education at an agricultural school called Ockham, which had been founded by Lady Byron, wife of the famous poet Lord Byron. While improving their literacy, they taught others manual skills. The Ockham superintendent offered the couple the positions of superintendent and matron of the school, but Ellen and William turned him down. Instead, William opened an importing business bringing in "fancy" goods, and Ellen continued to work as a seamstress.

They settled in West London, where they soon bought their own home which became a meeting place for abolitionists. The Crafts had four sons: Charles, Brougham, William, and Alfred; and a daughter they named Maria after Ellen's mother. Ellen had kept her promise that she would never bear children in slavery. In 1860, they became authors when their book, *Running a Thousand Miles for Freedom,* was published to great success.

William searched for and located his mother, and bought her freedom. He then found his sister and likewise freed and relocated her to be with her mother.

The next year William visited the king of Dahomey in West Africa, appealing to him to stop practicing human sacrifice. Because of the king's friendly reception, William returned to Dahomey in 1863 and lived there until 1867. William's efforts may have contributed to the end of slave trade in that country.

Ellen stayed home in London with the children during William's African sojourn and helped raise money for him to open a school in Sierra Leone. William also operated an import-export business with a British commercial house. The relations with the company deteriorated, though, and William had to leave Africa owing money to his employer.

While earning money to repay the company, William and Ellen also raised funds to help freed slaves in the United States. They developed a plan to buy a plantation in Georgia and operate it as a cooperative. Freed slaves who worked there would become independent farmers rather than continue to work in subservience to owners.

The freeing of slaves that followed the end of the Civil War opened the way for the Crafts to return home after nineteen years.

In 1870, with help from British supporters, they sailed to Boston. After some months, they bought a plantation a short distance from Savannah in South Carolina. Sadly, nightriders burned their first crop, and they had to sell the land and move back to Savannah to live with their oldest son, Charles.

Lacking funds to buy another piece of land, they leased Woodville Plantation, a farm of 1,800 acres at Ways Station in Bryan County, Georgia. There they opened the Woodville Cooperative Farm School. They spent all the money they had saved and took out a mortgage of $2,500 to build homes and a schoolhouse/church and to renovate the older buildings. They invited poor freed slaves to live there and to earn their keep with work. Their children went to the school where Tom and Ellen and their children taught. With help from Northern supporters, the Crafts bought Woodville in 1873.

By 1875 seventy-five pupils were enrolled in the school; thirty also lived on the property. Ellen would not allow teachers to whip children at the school. She told parents, "If you want to whip your own children, first go to the graveyard and pray."

Financial difficulties continued to plague the Crafts. In September 1876 a letter printed in Boston newspapers accused the couple of misusing school donations for their personal use. New York and Savannah papers reprinted the damaging letter. William lost the libel lawsuit he brought against the man who wrote the letter, and the Crafts' financial problems increased. Prices for farm crops were low at that time, so the farmers at Woodville earned little from their labors. Without sufficient funds, the school closed.

In the 1890s Ellen moved in with her daughter, who had married Dr. William Demos Crim, a physician who later became the U.S. minister to Liberia. Ellen died in 1891, and, at her request, her family buried her under her favorite tree on Woodville

Plantation. Later, in order to pay off a loan, William mortgaged the plantation. A few days after William's death in Charleston in January 1900, the plantation belonged to the mortgage holder.

Richard J. M. Blackett wrote: "Through their dramatic escape from Macon . . . the Crafts contributed to antebellum abolitionism in America and Britain. . . . Their decision to return to Georgia to work among the freedmen displayed both courage and a commitment to share in the future of their people."

REBECCA LATIMER FELTON
1835–1930

First Female U.S. Senator

*V*ice President Calvin Coolidge sounded the gavel at noon on Monday, November 20, 1922, calling the third session of the Sixty-Seventh United States Senate to order. The session lasted for only twelve minutes "out of respect for the memory of the deceased Senator Tom Watson" from Georgia.

Wrinkled, petite, eighty-seven-year-old Rebecca Felton, wearing gold-rimmed spectacles and her white hair piled on top of her head, sat beside Georgia Senator William J. Harris. She had come from her home in Cartersville, Georgia, expecting to be sworn in as a senator. She didn't know, however, if she would actually be allowed to take the oath. According to the *New York Times,* a few senators intended to oppose her being sworn in, fearful of the precedent that might be set for the election of other female senators.

Earlier that month, on November 8, 1922, Democrat Rebecca Felton had stood on the courthouse steps in Bartow County, Georgia, to be sworn in to fill the unexpired term of Tom Watson, a political friend. Georgia Governor Thomas W. Hardwick, who had voted against the Nineteenth Amendment while in the Sixty-fifth Congress, hoped that by allowing this appointment

Rebecca Latimer Felton

he could appease the ire of some of the women voters. He had decided to appoint a woman to complete the term, but only as a gesture; he knew a man would be chosen to succeed Watson on Election Day, so he thought Rebecca Felton would not actually spend any time in the Senate.

Walter F. George—indeed elected as Watson's successor, as Hardwick had predicted—could have taken over the position on November 20, but it seems Rebecca persuaded him to allow her to serve a couple of days in the Senate before he presented his credentials for official commission. That day, Senator Albert B. Cummins of Iowa presided in Coolidge's absence. After the commissioning of three new male senators, Georgia Senator Harris stood and spoke, "I hope no senator will object to [Mrs. Felton's] taking the oath of office [which] will not in any way prejudice Mr. George's claim to the seat to which the people of Georgia have elected him."

As predicted, Senator Thomas J. Walsh of Montana stood to express his objections on the grounds that Mrs. Felton's claims to the seat had ended with Walter George's election. The women who filled the gallery to see Mrs. Felton's swearing-in watched with anger. They felt that Senator Walsh was using a trumped-up charge to block a woman from becoming a senator.

None of the other senators rose in agreement with Walsh's arguments. The clerk then read Mrs. Felton's credentials, and the president pro tempore directed her to come to the rostrum to swear her oath.

Senator Harris escorted Mrs. Felton, who wore a floor-length black gown with a white lace collar and a black silk bonnet. She swore to uphold and defend the Constitution.

The women in the gallery broke a Senate rule by applauding enthusiastically, and the senators then joined them. The group clapped again when Senator B. P. (Pat) Harrison of Mississippi said, just before adjournment, "It augurs well for this session of Congress that . . . we should begin as we have today by seating a distinguished lady as the Senator from Georgia."

Since the body took care of no further business that day, Mrs. Felton did not get to record a "Yea" or "Nay" in Senate records. She asked to speak, but the schedule of the busy day did not permit it.

On Wednesday, November 22, Mrs. Felton answered "Present" at roll call and listened to a message from the House about the signing of three bills. She then rose and requested permission to speak. Cummins immediately recognized her as the "junior senator from Georgia."

Her remarks foreshadowed the future of women in Congress: "When the women of the country come in and sit with you, though there may be but a very few in the next few years, I pledge you that you will get ability, you will get integrity of purpose, you will get exalted patriotism, and you will get unstinted usefulness."

The last item of business the legislature took care of before the close of the morning session was Senate Resolution 366. That resolution directed the secretary of the senate "to pay the Honorable Rebecca Latimer Felton the amount due her as a Senator from the State of Georgia $287.67 for compensation from November 21 to 22, and $280 for mileage."

Rebecca Felton was the first woman to occupy a seat in the United States Senate and—at age eighty-seven—was also the oldest senator at the time. She also served the shortest term in the Senate's history. She actually served only one full day and until noon of a second day. After that, the newly elected Senator Walter George took over.

Born in 1835, Rebecca Felton grew up in a privileged situation. She admired her mother, Eleanor, and her father, Charles Latimer, owner of a plantation and slaves and owner of a tavern and general store in Decatur, northeast of Atlanta. She wrote: "My father was one of the staunchest and strongest of men, very much ahead of the time as to theories and thought—which accounts for my force of character and advanced ideas. Mother was the gentlest and most devout of women, imparting [to me] a religious ardor and stand in the temperance movement."

Rebecca's parents recognized and valued their firstborn's intelligence. Charles Latimer hired a tutor to start a small grammar school on the plantation when Rebecca was only five. She always did well in her studies, excelling in music and art. When the tutor left, Charles Latimer sent Rebecca to a private school at the local Presbyterian church. From there, Rebecca went to Madison Female College, a strict Methodist school in Madison, Georgia.

In her graduating class in 1852, Rebecca A. Latimer had three distinctions: She was among the rare Southern females who received a classical liberal arts education; she had the highest grades in her class; and at age seventeen she was the youngest member of the class of twelve.

She had one accomplishment in common with Dr. William H. Felton, who delivered the "literary address" at her commencement. He had also graduated first in his class. The speaker took special note of the young valedictorian, and the two began courting.

Twenty-nine-year-old Dr. Felton was a widower, his first wife having died in childbirth. He had served in the Georgia General Assembly from 1851 to 1852 and had started a medical practice in Cartersville in northwest Georgia in 1847, but he had developed a neurological disorder similar to palsy, a generative form of Parkinson's disease that strained his nervous system. He left the practice to become a farmer and to be ordained as a Methodist minister. He would serve the church in various positions for almost fifty years, but he declined to receive any pay.

The couple married on October 11, 1853, at Rebecca's parents' white-columned plantation home. Dr. Felton then took his bride to live on his family's one thousand–acre farm 100 miles away in northwest Georgia. Dr. Felton's parents still lived there, and father and son worked a very successful farm. In 1860, William Felton's total assets were valued at $14,000; his real estate had a value of $5,000. Today those amounts would read approximately $280,000 and $100,000 respectively. Dr. Felton's father had total assets of $25,000, which included $12,000 worth of real estate. The two men jointly owned fifty slaves.

Dr. Felton admired his wife's active mind and independent spirit. He was unusual for husbands of that day in that he believed that women should be included in the world of new ideas and public activities.

William and Rebecca had three children between 1853 and 1861. First came John Latimer Felton. Even though William had medical training, he couldn't prevent the death of their one-year-old daughter, Mary Eleanor, from dysentery in 1857. In 1859 William Harrell, Jr., joined the family. Rebecca practiced music while raising her children with the help of slaves.

The Feltons, along with their neighbors, suffered a great deal when the Civil War came in 1861. In his article, "William & Rebecca Felton: The Dynamic Duo of Political Reform," Richard Thornton wrote, "Their experiences are remarkably similar to the plot of Margaret Mitchell's *Gone with the Wind.* William wanted to secede but Rebecca did not, but when Georgia seceded from the Union in January 1861, she accepted the fact."

William Felton, now thirty-eight years old and growing increasingly incapacitated by palsy, did not enter the military, but he continued to farm. He and Rebecca provided medical services for wounded soldiers as they passed through nearby Cartersville by train.

In the spring of 1864, when Union troops moved farther south into Georgia, the family left their farm in the care of fifteen slaves and took refuge on a rented farm in the central part of the state, bringing with them some slaves and all their cattle and farm implements. William and Rebecca and their sons, Johnny, ten, and William, five, lived in a pine shack while the slaves lived in lean-tos or tents. While there, Dr. Felton attended to ill soldiers and civilians in a Macon hospital.

"At this point," wrote Thornton, "the Feltons' lives entered a horrific period, seemingly scripted by Margaret Mitchell." In the fall of 1864, Union troops invaded central Georgia and took all the food they could find, including cattle. The appearance of Confederate cavalry stopped the raid, but what the Union soldiers left behind dealt further blows. They infected Georgia citizens and slaves with red measles. All of the Feltons were undernourished, and seven in their group succumbed to the disease, including young William H. Felton, Jr.

While Rebecca was still grieving, she received word that her mother was near death at a relative's home in northeast Georgia, a victim of another disease introduced by Federal troops. Rebecca's attempt to take a train was foiled because of the destruction of a bridge by the invading army. She took off in a wagon pulled by a mule. When she encountered Union troops, she had to return to her temporary home. Rebecca's mother died without seeing her daughter.

Later that year, the Feltons had to leave their rented farm because it lay in General William T. Sherman's path as he was conducting his march to the sea. They spent the following six months in a refugee camp in southern Georgia. They ate only what they could get from hunting and fishing, nearly starving to death. They lost their last remaining child, Johnny, to malaria that summer. William and Rebecca also nearly died of fever.

The Civil War ended in April 1865. Like Scarlett O'Hara returning to Tara in *Gone with the Wind,* the Feltons returned to their home late in 1865. To secure the cost of traveling by train, including paying freight for the boys' caskets, Rebecca sold their handsome paneled carriage, which had cost six hundred dollars in gold before the war, for only one hundred dollars in greenbacks.

They found wholesale destruction when they arrived back at their farm. Thornton wrote: "During Sherman's invasion of northwest Georgia, both Union and Confederate soldiers had torn down fences and outbuildings to build cooking fires. It was standard operating procedure for the Union troops to burn all stores, mills, public buildings, farm outbuildings and even houses known to belong to Confederate officers."

The Felton home still stood, but stragglers and bushwhackers had damaged what the soldiers had left. The Feltons, both in poor health, had no money. Rebecca Felton made a promise similar to the one Scarlett O'Hara made: "I will never be poor again."

During the Reconstruction years, William made little money on the farm. Few schools existed in Georgia following the war, so the couple opened Felton Academy in early 1866 in rented space in nearby Cartersville. The school attracted eighty students; the Feltons were the only faculty.

The Feltons had two more sons: Howard Erwin Felton was born in 1869 and Paul Aiken Felton followed in 1871. Tragedy soon plagued the family again, however. Young Paul died two years later of dysentery.

When the Ladies Aid Society was formed to help disabled Confederate veterans and war widows, Rebecca joined. When she later became president, some locals objected, feeling that the Feltons had contributed little to the war effort.

In 1874, after Reconstruction ended, William re-entered politics in what has been remembered as one of Georgia's bitterest campaigns. He ran as an Independent for the congressional seat of the Seventh District, where feeling was strong against radical Republicans. Rebecca campaigned extensively for her husband. She told an *Atlanta Constitution* reporter:

> I was shot into politics. . . . I wrote hundreds of letters all over fourteen counties . . . and for two months before the close kept a man and a horse at the door to catch every mail train three miles away. . . . At one time my health broke down, but I was propped up in bed with pillows and wrote ahead. I made appointments for speaking, recruited speakers, answered newspaper attacks, contracted for the printing and distribution of circulars and sample ballots, and more than all, kept a brave face to the fore and a smiling face to the almost exhausted candidate.

William's critics used his lack of military experience against him, but he nevertheless won the election. Rebecca served as her husband's private secretary, general counselor, campaign manager, and press secretary when he served in the Georgia state legislature and for his four campaigns for the U.S. House of Representatives. She especially loved their life in "Washington City," where she learned to draft bills, address mass meetings, and correspond with constituents. By assisting in writing and editing her husband's speeches, Rebecca helped him become known nationally as an out-standing orator. The public viewed her as the most politically informed Congressman's wife from the South.

Rebecca ruffled many feathers with her aggressive behavior, though. She did not sit quietly at home as people expected a Southern lady to do. During the hot summers and falls of 1876 and 1878, she traveled around the district with Dr. Felton in a custom-made buggy, attending political rallies. That brought her special criticism because men considered such rallies to be too crass for feminine participation. Rebecca used her femininity in a particular way, giving out information at teas and coffee hours in hotels or piazzas when her husband felt too tired to meet with constituents. The work of the couple blended so much that admirers called Rebecca "our Second Representative from the Seventh." One critical editorial asked, "Which Felton Is the Congressman and Which the Wife?"

Unfortunately, many of William's supporters suffered in their businesses because of their connection with him, and he was voted out of office in 1880.

Next, the couple focused on improving their farm. They also started a weekly newspaper called the *Cartersville Free Press*. Rebecca wrote articles denouncing abuses in the state prison system, especially the confinement of men, women, and juveniles together. She saw the fruit of her labors some years later when the groups began to be housed separately. Recognizing that alcoholism caused many of the problems of families in Georgia, she joined the Women's Christian Temperance Union and supported their fight against the evils of strong drink. She achieved stature as a speaker on women's issues and wrote regular articles for the editorial pages of several major Southern newspapers.

William Felton returned to politics in 1884, winning three terms in the state assembly. By this time, people accepted the fact that Rebecca was his political partner.

Rebecca's managerial skills led her to virtually take over control of the farm operations, including William's finances; if they disagreed on what should be done, she did it her way. She increased their landholdings, buying nearby farms; she even became an insurance agent and had a railroad spur built on their land to open iron mines.

William already had national recognition, but Rebecca achieved it in 1893 when she became president of the Ladies Managing Board of the World's Columbian Exposition held in Chicago. Northern protests removed her from that position, but in Atlanta in 1894, she became Chairman of the Executive Board of the Cotton States International Exposition of 1895. That same year, the Georgia Training School for Girls made her a trustee.

William retired from politics in 1896 at the age of seventy-three, and the couple later moved into Cartersville. Rebecca's political activity took a new direction. In 1899 she began writing a column for the *Semi-Weekly Edition*, the rural edition of the *Atlanta Journal*. Speaking out on everything from farm life to Confederate pensions, she influenced thousands of readers across rural Georgia and the Southeast. Her column, "The Country Home," ran regularly for ten years.

By 1907 William could barely walk or speak. He remained bedridden—almost in a vegetative state—until his death on September 24, 1909.

Rebecca continued working on the causes dear to her heart, especially women's right to vote, the Progressive Movement, free public education, the admittance of women to the state university, and criminal justice reform. In 1915, partly due to Mrs. Felton's twenty-five years of efforts, the Georgia Training School for Girls in Atlanta allowed poor white girls to receive vocational training.

In early 1900, believing that women political leaders would lift the moral level of the people, Mrs. Felton joined the suffrage movement. Although friends cautioned her to "avoid collisions," she plunged heartily ahead, expressing advanced views on many social and political issues. The public had gained a deep respect for her and her viewpoints over the years, and newspapers that had attacked her earlier now invited her to write for them.

Mrs. Felton shared the anti-Negro prejudice of rural Georgians at that time. She begrudged African Americans heading north, wishing they would stay and pick cotton instead.

In 1911 her book *Memoirs of Georgia Politics* came out and, in 1919, her second book, *Country Life in Georgia in the Days of My Youth*, was released.

Rebecca's support of women's suffrage and her contacts with national women leaders did not please members of the Temperance Movement, but respect for her grew nationwide. The Progressive Movement in Georgia made her chairman of the Women's Auxiliary of the Progressive Party and in 1912 made her a delegate to the "Bull Moose" Party Convention. Rebecca was an isolationist, and her political articles in 1920 objected to Woodrow Wilson's foreign policy and to the League of Nations. These articles helped elect Watson as senator and Hardwick as governor, both isolationists. In 1921 her efforts for women's suffrage—along with those of many others around the country—paid off when women received the right to vote. President Harding invited her to serve as the only woman on his Advisory Committee.

When she spoke to the state legislature of Georgia in November 1921, it was the first time in the state's history that a woman had addressed that body. Assembly President Clark Howell introduced her with this statement: "There is a great deal of discussion and contention as to who is the smartest man in Georgia, but it is universally contended that the woman who is to address you today is the brightest and smartest woman in the state."

After her very short stint in the Senate in 1922, Rebecca received another distinctive honor when she became the first woman to receive a postgraduate degree—an honorary doctorate of letters—from the University of Georgia. She continued to write articles for newspapers. Two years later, she moved into her son's home in Cartersville.

Rebecca Latimer Felton died of pneumonia in Atlanta on January 25, 1930, at age ninety-five while attending a trustee's meeting of the Georgia Training School for Girls. Her body resides beside her husband's in a mausoleum in a Cartersville cemetery.

At the time of her death, she was still writing, advocating for her favorite causes, and managing her own business affairs. In his biography of Rebecca, John E. Talmadge wrote, ". . . from 1835 to 1930, . . . [she] was perhaps the best-known woman in Georgia. Few Georgians have had a hand in so much of their state's history."

An *Atlanta Journal* article noted:

> Her mind never neutral, flashed in great battles; her heart throbbed high to the march of epoch-making ideas; her spirit called like a trumpet to those about her to fight the good fight and to keep the faith. . . . Her name is graven in the history of the commonwealth she loved and in the hearts of those who knew her best.

MARY ELLEN "NELLIE" PETERS BLACK

1851–1919

Mover and Shaker

*A*ttractive eighteen-year-old Nellie Peters returned to her Atlanta home after graduating from the prestigious finishing school, Miss Maria Eastman's Brooke Hall, in Media, Pennsylvania, ready to serve her community. The school educated the daughters of America's most privileged families.

Probably due to the influence and example of both of her parents, Nellie developed an early desire for service. Her father, Richard Peters, offered her a diamond ring as a graduation present. Nellie's answer reflected her personality and was predictive of her future: she declined, asking for a saddle horse instead. It was on this black horse, which she named Diamond, that she later rode to do her charitable work among the city's disadvantaged in the slums, long before women began to organize for such work.

Nellie was born Mary Ellen Peters in 1851. Different sources list her as "the oldest of eight children," "the second child of seven children," and "the second of nine, the first daughter." We can conclude that she grew up in a large family. Her father was one of Atlanta's most successful businessmen. A civil engineer, he

Mary Ellen Peters Black with her daughters, Louise King Black and
Mrs. Lamar C. Rucker.

had come to Georgia from his home state of Pennsylvania in February 1835 with only one hundred dollars he had borrowed from his aunt.

Richard achieved the American dream. Among other accomplishments, he helped build the Georgia Railroad and became the company's general manager in 1837. When the price of railroad shares dropped sharply in the panic of 1840, he bought a large number of shares that later added to his wealth.

Through Richard's efforts, the name of the town Marthasville changed to the present Atlanta. He had many interests, and he turned all of them into moneymaking ventures. After resigning from his position with the railroad, he bought a stagecoach line that operated from Madison, Georgia, to Montgomery, Alabama. He bought real estate, much of it located in present-day Atlanta, an investment that paid off handsomely. The capitol of Georgia sits on land he bought and then sold for a profit.

Richard Peters met Mary Jane Thompson, who at fifteen was noted as "one of the prettiest young women in Georgia." The two married on February 18, 1848, when she was sixteen years old and he was thirty-five. They had a happy marriage and were among Atlanta's outstanding citizens. Richard Peters bought one of the city's most prominent homes, set among two acres of outstanding gardens. The orchard was in the rear, and Richard bought ten additional acres on which to pasture his cows.

Richard took an interest in agriculture and bought a farm in North Georgia. He conducted experiments in livestock breeding, bringing Jersey cows and Angora goats from abroad. His interest in horticulture led to the opening of his nursery in Atlanta. Before the Civil War, he shipped four thousand young trees to California via Cape Horn.

Nellie grew up in comfort with four servants to help take care of her. Her family, devout Episcopalians, attended St. Philip's church every Sunday.

Nellie, nine years old when the Civil War broke out, was exposed at an early age to the horrors of the war. She saw firsthand the destruction of the city. Nellie began her "apprenticeship" in service to others under her mother's tutelage. In Mrs. Peters's carriage, the only one in town, they visited some of the temporary military hospitals. As Nellie accompanied her mother, she was observing, absorbing, and learning. She developed a keen desire to help the needy, learning that personal wealth was not to be used for personal pleasure only but for the good of those less fortunate.

In *Richard Peters: Champion of the New South*, Royce Shingleton wrote:

> The magnitude of the task of caring for the infirm soldiers is suggested by the figures: eighty thousand sick and wounded in Atlanta during the war, of whom five thousand died. The influx turned Atlanta into "a dreary succession of canteens for soup and coffee, greasy ladles, ever-swarming flies, and bearded, smelly, terribly hurt men." The work of the women was magnificent. One of the most important organizations to relieve the suffering was the St. Philips Hospital Aid Society, established in affiliation with the Georgia Relief and Hospital Association. . . . The group distributed supplies in Atlanta sent from many parts of the South. Mary Jane Peters, a leading member, made donations to the society; visited the hospitals daily, usually with her daughter, Nellie, and household slave, Mose, who carried on his arm a hamper filled with food . . . ; and she provided kettles of hot coffee to the soldiers as they arrived in the city. But her most difficult duty was speaking words of comfort and reading the Bible to the dying in their last hours, and then writing letters to their families.

During this time, the Peters family had its own personal grief when two of Nellie's younger siblings died.

The energetic Mr. Peters had yet another venture going as a blockade-runner during the war. Through that avenue, he brought in abundant supplies of food. Mary Jane Peters later wrote: "In that way we could help others. It was my pleasure to go each day in the carriage with my baby and nurse, and carry cans of fresh buttermilk, baskets of cakes and biscuit to the hospitals and send kettles of hot coffee when needed for the sick and wounded soldiers as they arrived in the city."

In her notes on Nellie Peters Black, Nita Black Rucker wrote, "On July 9, 1864 the northern sky glowed red in the predawn darkness enveloping Atlanta. Suddenly, a pounding on the door shattered the slumber of the Richard Peters household at the corner of Mitchell and Forsyth streets. Peters opened the door." A member of the governor's staff had sent a middle-of-the-night message that the Federals were burning the bridge over the Chattahoochee River and that those troops would soon be in the city. Mrs. Peters left Atlanta hastily with the children that day on a train to Augusta, Georgia, to stay in the home of a friend. Mr. Peters remained behind, joining his family in mid-August.

Nellie's name became well known through a legend started by Dr. Charles T. Quintard, a physician and minister who served as a chaplain in the Army of Tennessee. He sought refuge in Atlanta and preached to other Episcopalian refugees in a theater. He enlisted Richard Peters's help in securing funds to build a new parish that came to be named St. Luke's and was built by Confederate military labor. Mary Jane donated a pair of silver goblets for the altar.

At this time, General William Tecumseh Sherman's army especially targeted Atlanta's churches for destruction. According to the legend, one day in August, Dr. Quintard found Nellie's handkerchief in St. Luke's. Nellie had dropped it during her infant brother Stephen's funeral in June 1864. During the later shelling of the city, an explosive ripped into the church, breaking the prayer desk. A large Bible fell upon the device, smothering it. The church was spared at that time, but Sherman's armies later destroyed it.

Finding the handkerchief inspired Dr. Quintard to write a booklet called "Nellie Peters's Pocket Handkerchief and What It Saw," describing the horrors of the city's siege. He sent the handkerchief to Nellie in Augusta.

After the war ended, the family returned to Atlanta. Although their home still stood while many others near it had burned, it had sustained shell damage. Luckily, Richard Peters's farsightedness in his business ventures helped to preserve his fortune at a time when many other families suffered great losses.

Needy people filled the city. Royce Shingleton wrote:

Private relief was more popular but usually seasonal, operating only during the winter months. Fairs, lectures, and suppers provided funds for the poor. Mary Jane and Nellie, resuming the active social life of the Peters family, helped organize the especially popular calico balls to which women wore calico dresses and men wore extremely long scarves. On the day following the ball, all the calico material was donated to the poor in addition to merchants' contributions of coal, wood, cloth, and other useful material. . . . From these calico balls grew the capable Ladies Relief Society.

Nellie, an eligible young woman, did not marry right out of school or make homemaking her career as most of her peers did. She must have turned one man down more than once because he wrote from Augusta on February 20, 1871: ". . . I regret it very much [declining an invitation to her "Charity Party"] as nothing would have given me more pleasure than to have renewed our long, dissolved engagement by the re-re-redelivery of the diamond ring and the plighting of my troth again."

During the 1870s Nellie began her charity work among Atlanta's slum residents and started a Sunday school in that part of town. During the week, she visited the sick and needy. Richard Peters as well apparently had a mind for helping the unfortunate, because in 1872 he donated a great deal of money for his church to build Holy Innocents Chapel—Atlanta's first mission of the Episcopal Church—for the residents living in the slums. For the next five years, Nellie worked there.

Nellie chose to marry in 1877 when she responded to the charms of Colonel George Robinson Black. A friend wrote her, "I am prepared to fall in love myself with Col. Black after your impartial description of him. If he is only a quarter as nice as you are I will be quite satisfied." Col. Black—actually an attorney and a member of the Georgia legislature—had received his honorary military title during the war, as did many other men. Nellie became not only a bride of a man sixteen years her senior but also a stepmother: Black, a widower, had four children only slightly younger than Nellie. The family lived in Col. Black's home in Sylvania, Georgia. The couple later had three children of their own: Nita Hughes in 1878, Louise King in 1879, and Ralph Peters in 1881. They donated the land on which the first Episcopal church in Sylvania was built.

In 1881 Colonel Black was elected as a representative to the U.S. Congress, so the family moved to Washington, D.C. In 1882 Col. Black suffered a stroke; he died in 1886. Nellie continued to manage the family farm and raise the children. Two years after her husband's death, Nellie brought her children back to Atlanta to live in her parents' new home on the famous Peachtree Street, an avenue lined with mansions.

Because of Nellie's family's wealth and social prominence, she could have always lived her life in a shallow, self-indulgent way. In the late 1880s, widowed and with seven children to raise, she had even more reason to spend all her time on her own concerns. However, she immediately set about serving the community as she always had. Her wealth allowed her to hire help in her home so she could be free to work in the community.

The Episcopal Diocese of Georgia organized a Women's Auxiliary, and Nellie became its first president. In 1889, she became president of a benevolent society called the King's Daughters. By 1890, she had organized the King's Daughters Hospital, one of the first charity hospitals in Atlanta. As the city grew and needed a larger medical institution, Nellie helped found Grady Hospital, currently Atlanta's largest charity hospital.

In 1890, Nellie revived the defunct Holy Innocents Mission by getting permission to reopen the mission in an empty store. On Sunday afternoons, Nellie and her children, who assisted her with music, taught the children of a poor section of Atlanta.

When plans were being laid for the Cotton States International Exposition to be held in 1895 in Atlanta, Nellie was appointed chairman of the nursery and hospital committee of the Women's Department. She secured donations of furniture and supplies as well as the services of twenty volunteer physicians. When the world came to the Expo, the volunteers treated 2,085 patients in the hospital and examined more than 1,000 babies.

The exhibition on kindergartens housed in the Woman's Building caught Nellie's eye. She wanted kindergartens for Atlanta's children. In 1896 she and a group founded the Atlanta Free Kindergarten Association, with Nellie as its president, a position she held until 1911. Using funds raised by different organizations, the group opened its first kindergarten near a cotton mill. Prominent Atlantans grew accustomed to receiving letters each Christmas from Nellie asking for donations to sustain the program.

In 1896, when the Federation of the Atlanta Woman's Club organized with Nellie as a charter member, she represented the

Atlanta Free Kindergarten Association. She served as the organization's chairman of the kindergarten committee for many years. In 1904 Nellie wrote for the *Atlanta Journal*: "A liberal public has ever been ready to lend a helping hand in the support of the schools' now six schools, with an enrollment of 350 pupils, are the result of this generous assistance." In her visits to five public schools, she found four hundred pupils who had benefited from the kindergartens.

She continued: "The teachers spoke of them as being among their best pupils—and it has proved most conclusively that our claim is a just one. The better a child's mind is prepared for school, the better results you will obtain—just as any farmer will tell you never to plant your seed until the soil is well prepared."

In 1906 the Atlanta Free Kindergarten Association became affiliated with the Georgia Federation of Women's Clubs. The efforts of that committee resulted in seventy-six kindergartens being started throughout the state by 1912. Although a bill introduced into the state legislature that year to provide kindergartens in all public schools did not pass, Nellie continued to promote the measure. Her work bore fruit several years later. Shortly after her death in 1919, the Atlanta public schools opened citywide kindergartens.

Meanwhile, Nellie kept busy in other areas. In 1889 her father died, and Nellie made trips to North Georgia to manage his farm. The farm came to be known as the best managed in North Georgia. She studied horticulture, and when she served as chair of the agriculture committee of the Georgia Federation of Women's Clubs, she put that knowledge to use.

After the nation entered World War I, Nellie instructed the club to follow President Woodrow Wilson's urgings to preserve foodstuffs. When Nellie learned that Georgia imported two million dollars worth of food annually, that fact gave her additional incentive to support the effort. Federation clubs joined the state department of agriculture and the University of Georgia in enlisting the help of farm demonstration agents throughout the state to teach the needed skills.

Nellie did her part by speaking to more than nineteen thousand people at agricultural rallies over a three-year period. Her 5,000 miles of travel and the fifty articles she wrote for newspapers earned her the title "Dollar a Year" woman from President Wilson in 1917. These efforts earned her the title "War President" within the Federation, and her broader efforts led to the establishment of 4-H clubs for farm youth.

In addition to its war efforts, the Federation campaigned against illiteracy in 1915. Nellie, a persuasive speaker, addressed the General Assembly of Georgia, urging them to pass a law requiring compulsory education. That law passed the next year. She took her powers of persuasion to the University of Georgia, urging the full admittance of women, which the university made a rule in 1919. She later used her influence to get women lawyers admitted to the Georgia state bar.

In 1916, at the age of sixty-five, with the energy one might expect of a much younger woman, Nellie became president of the Georgia Federation of Women's Clubs, the position that led to her most lasting and extensive achievements.

Her work during the next few years drew the attention of people outside Georgia and brought honors and more work. In 1916 she was appointed president of the Conference of Southern Women; and in 1918 she was selected as a delegate to the Win the War for Permanent Peace convention. In that same year, she was made honorary chairperson of the Women's Council of the National Defense, Georgia Division; and in 1919 she was selected as a delegate for the southern conference for the League of Nations.

It is hard to believe that one woman had the energy or the time to do more, but Nellie did. Her love of farming led her to work toward agricultural reform. In her capacity as a member of the agriculture committee of the Georgia Federation of Women's Clubs, she organized a series of rallies in the twelve state districts. Nellie had the skill of delegation, so she called on the clubwomen within the districts to recruit people to attend the rallies. Experts from the College of Agriculture at the University of Georgia and from the various government agencies cooperating with the state agencies spoke at these meetings. Within six months, every agency for agricultural development in the state had asked for the cooperation of the clubwomen.

When the General Federation of Women's Clubs decided to honor a former member at their Golden Jubilee Celebration, they chose Nellie as "outstanding member of the national federation." While they listed her many achievements, they stated that her most lasting contribution was the establishment of a free kindergarten system throughout the state.

In addition to her civic work, Nellie belonged to several social organizations: the Daughters of the American Revolution, the Pioneer Women of Atlanta, the United Daughters of the Confederacy, and the Colonial Dames.

Nellie died on August 4, 1919, at her Atlanta home from "acute cardiac dilatation." Her last words were, "Tell everybody I love them."

In an *Atlanta Magazine* article, "City Shapers," in 1976, the publication named her as one of two hundred persons "who have contributed most to the character and look of Metro-Atlanta." Another later article in that magazine named her as one of Georgia's Twenty-Five Historic Mothers.

JULIETTE GORDON LOW

1860–1927

America's First Girl Scout

*I*n *Lady From Savannah*, Denny Shultz and Daisy Gordon Lawrence wrote:

> Of the five Gordon children who lived to maturity, Daisy [Juliette] was the one who became world famous—and the one who felt that her personal life was a tragic failure. And anyone who knew her could not have imagined that at middle age, she would reverse her lifelong habits of spending her time and energies on her recreations and use that vivacity to organize the Girl Scouts.

Daisy's forebears undoubtedly contributed to her unique personality. The Gordons had been stalwart Savannah residents for two centuries before Daisy was born. Her grandfather, William Washington Gordon, had served several terms as Savannah's mayor; his statue stands in the city today. A great uncle, a Justice of the United States Supreme Court, built the Gordon mansion in 1821.

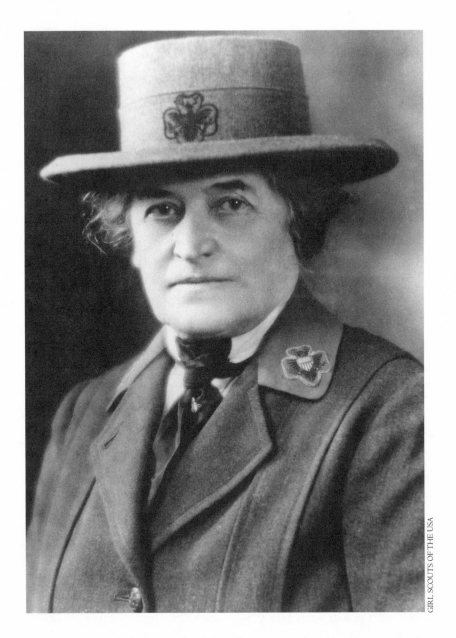

Juliette Gordon Low

Then William Washington Gordon II shook up the Gordon clan when he brought home his Chicago-born bride, Nellie Kinzie. Nellie had caught Willie's eye when she slid down the banister of the Yale library staircase and knocked off his hat, which had been on the newel post. Nellie had descended from high-spirited men and women. Her great-grandmother, Eleanor Lytle Kinzie, had been captured by Indians and lived among them in the Midwest for four years. Her grandfather had built the first house in Chicago, and for twenty years his family had been the only white family in northern Illinois, except for the families of Fort Dearborn personnel. Nellie's father spoke seventeen different Indian languages. As the town of Chicago grew in the Midwestern wilderness, Nellie's mother and grandmother were among the city's most distinguished women.

Willie and Nellie married on December 21, 1857. Eleanor was their first child. Juliette, the second, was born on October 31, 1860. Her parents named her after her grandmother, Juliette Kinzie, and nicknamed her Daisy to avoid confusion.

When the Civil War started, Willie immediately volunteered for military service. While the war raged, life in the South became very difficult. Pregnant Nellie and her daughters lost weight and were sick due to lack of food. Yankees invaded Savannah, and General William T. Sherman called on Nellie to provide social activities for himself and his staff. The officers especially liked witty young Daisy. When Confederate officers' families received orders to evacuate Savannah, General Sherman provided an escort for Nellie and the girls to travel to Chicago.

On the trip, Daisy, then four, contracted what was called brain fever; her life hung by a thread. Her doctor warned her family that others should do as Daisy said so she wouldn't become overly excited. Years later her family would wonder if that was the beginning of Daisy's lifelong stubbornness and disregard for the advice of others.

The Gordons experienced near poverty after they returned to Savannah following the war. They had a son named William Washington, called Bill, and another daughter, Mabel. Willie opened a cotton brokerage business, and gradually the family's economic situation improved.

Daisy continued to display her considerable wit, and she rode horses, swam, and played tennis well. But she was extremely disorganized. She often lost her possesions and usually blamed others for those losses. Shultz and Lawrence wrote, "Her mind simply did not work like that of the average person . . . through all her life . . . she could not understand why her reasoning methods and actions were considered strange . . . her conversation was strewn with malapropisms. . . . Daisy . . . did everything from her heart . . . Any person or animal in distress evoked a flood of sympathy, and she rushed in to do something. . . ."

Daisy's brother Arthur described his sister thus:

It is difficult to describe her with any accuracy because she was so many-sided and unexpected and incalculable. There was nothing conventional or tepid or neutral about her. She had an eager desire to realize life to its utmost, and she would try anything, particularly if she had never attempted it before. What she enjoyed, she enjoyed to her very finger tips; and one reason why she was so eagerly sought after lay in the fact that she was not only very entertaining and amusing when she desired to be, but she was frequently killingly funny when she had no intention of being funny at all.

Eleanor Arnett Nash, Ogden Nash's sister, wrote that Daisy "had a wicked wit, and a charm I am too word-poor to describe. She was quicksilver and pepper—the whole leavened with humanity and laugher. She was the person I most liked to be with."

In the summer Nellie sent her children to an aunt's house in North Georgia to get them away from Savannah's heat and the threat of yellow fever and malaria. There the Gordon children could play with a brood of cousins. At these gatherings Daisy revealed a talent for mimicry, acting, and writing and directing plays.

When Daisy turned thirteen, she joined her older sister at Stuart Hall, a boarding school in Virginia where the students could speak only in French or German. She revealed talents for drawing and French before transferring to another boarding school, Edge Hill, also in Virginia. Though she behaved badly and received demerits while there, she excelled in drawing and managed to graduate. At graduation, she received a medal for drawing rather than for scholastics, which disappointed her. Daisy then entered Mesdemoiselles Charbonier's, a finishing school in New York City, where she studied French and oil painting.

In the summer of 1874, at the age of fourteen, Daisy formed the Helpful Hands, an organization for young girls. The plan called for the girls to sew articles to give to the poor. Since Daisy herself didn't know how to sew, her siblings called the club the "Helpless Hands."

Around 1880 Daisy was introduced to society. She was surprised to find that many young men considered her pretty. Her beauty coupled with her ready wit made her quite a belle. Her ambitions extended no further than to marry a rich man and move in society.

In December 1880 Daisy's younger sister Alice died from scarlet fever. Daisy found some solace in her religious beliefs, which deepened. She entered into a new relationship with her mother, declaring her independence more strongly and essentially becoming a mother to her mother, who grieved deeply.

Two years later, with his wife still grieving, Willie decided his daughters needed to move on with their lives. He sent Daisy, then twenty-two years old, to Europe for the first time. She visited the Andrew Low family in Scotland. Here she met the Low's son, Willy McKay Low, but she did not disclose this to her family. The next year, Willy and Daisy met in Savannah.

Soon Daisy started her pattern of traveling. Shultz and Lawrence wrote:

> And this was to be Daisy's life pattern from now on. We shall make no effort to trace her wanderings, for our story would become a mere tabulation of departures and arrivals. Until she married and settled, as far as Daisy ever settled, in England, she was shuttling back and forth between friends and relatives in the North . . . and . . . in the South, alighting in Savannah at intervals, to entertain her Northern friends in her turn with a round of parties. Soon, though, she would be off again on her endless quest for gaiety and pleasure. . . .

Although Daisy was now in her mid-twenties and usually distant from her parents, they kept tight rein on her contacts with young men.

In the summer of 1884, Daisy made her second trip to Europe, spending part of the time with the Lows. She did not mention Willy Low in her letters home. A letter to her brother Bill two years later, though, revealed that she and Willy had been in love for four years and were "as good as engaged."

Why would Daisy, always truthful, have withheld this information from her family? Willie Gordon scorned men who lived on inherited wealth rather than working, and he did not hesitate to order his daughters to break up with men who did not meet his approval. Love led Daisy to behave in an atypical manner.

Fun-loving Daisy fell in love with a "beautiful" man, according to her description. Tall, slender, blond, with deep-set blue eyes, Willy Low had been compared by others to a Greek god. Willy was heir to a multimillion dollar fortune, a family wealth unusual even in the United States. He knew the Prince of Wales, who would become Edward VII, and mingled with beautiful, charming women. Shultz and Lawrence wrote: "He had been in and out of amorous entanglements, adored by women. . . . Daisy's artlessness and sincerity presumably appealed to him more than her wit and charm, for he set no great value on wit and moved in circles where the women were adept at making themselves pleasant."

After Mrs. Low's death, Willy's older sisters had raised him, spoiling him terribly. His wealth spared him from training for any career. Willie Gordon did not approve of the match between his daughter and Low, and Daisy likewise feared that Willy's father would forbid the marriage.

Willy Low planned to visit Daisy in Savannah. Shortly before his arrival date, Daisy had an earache. She insisted that the doctor inject nitrate of silver into her ear to relieve the pain, a treatment she had read that New York doctors were using. Daisy remained nearly deaf in that ear for the rest of her life as a result of that treatment. Due to his disapproval, Willie Gordon would not allow Willy Low to see his daughter when he arrived.

The elderly Mr. Low gave his approval for the marriage in the spring of 1885, and Willie Gordon finally agreed also. The young couple planned to live in the Lows' Savannah home. That summer, Andrew Low died, and Willy inherited his fortune. Daisy and Willy were married in Christ Church on December 21, her parents' wedding day. The Gordon family christened the new husband "Billow," to eliminate confusion with Willie and Bill Gordon. As the couple left the church, a grain of rice thrown by a guest lodged in Daisy's good ear. The doctor who removed it damaged the eardrum permanently, and she lost all hearing in that ear.

The young couple settled in one of the grand homes of the city and gave equally grand parties. That summer, they left for England, where Billow rented two homes for them. Daisy, who had eighteen servants to assist her, spent her time having fun. The couple took part in the social life of the upper class: house parties, balls, dinners, luncheons, and opera and theater parties. Billow owned his own racing horse.

Shultz and Lawrence wrote:

> . . . if Willie and Nellie had known from the beginning the position Daisy was to occupy, they could not have given her better training for it. She had been well-schooled in social graces. . . . Her parents had given her freedom after her years of formal schooling to move in high social circles in the North as well as in the South, and to accustom herself to different practices and mores. Her outdoor accomplishments . . . were precisely the ones most useful to her in her new life, while her talent for gracious entertaining . . . enabled her to take her place at once as a successful hostess. . . . Her love of gaiety . . . fitted her . . . to find zest in every ball and every dinner.

Even though she was an animal lover, she rode the hounds on foxhunts. Later she fell and strained a shoulder. She felt a loss at having to give up that recreation.

Shortly after the marriage, doctors told Daisy she could never have children. Daisy grieved for the rest of her life over that inability.

The Lows eventually owned four homes, and Daisy became occupied with furnishing them. Billow took Daisy to Egypt, her first trip there.

When the Lows returned to England, Daisy went to Paris to buy a white satin gown to wear for presentation at court. In the coming months, people in the highest levels of British society dined at the Low residence. Daisy wore beautiful clothes and expensive jewelry while presiding over a table filled with delicious fare. She introduced American dishes that her parents sent: hams, sweet potatoes, corn, and pickles and such.

Daisy's family visited, leading to a lifelong closeness between herself and her brother Arthur. Her sister Mabel's visit led to Mabel's marriage to an Englishman and her settlement in England. Nellie and Willie visited also. Each winter, Daisy and Mabel returned to Savannah for a busy time of visiting friends.

Daisy's deafness proved burdensome, but typical of her style, she turned that defect into an asset. Unable to hear what others said, she developed the habit of doing most of the talking, usually provoking laughter. She treated others with respect and importance, though, so no one saw her as egotistical. Since she couldn't hear others' opinions, she became more and more an individualist, doing what she wanted to do. Sometimes she wound up in embarrassing circumstances, but she had a way of turning those into amusing incidents.

Billow didn't want his wife to do charity work that would take her into the slums, so Daisy sought out other individuals and places where she could help. For example, she regularly visited a workhouse to cheer up the inmates.

After Daisy had to give up riding, she found herself alone a great deal, as Billow continued to pursue his active social life. Daisy returned to her artwork, first carving a mantelpiece in their home, then doing oil paintings. Although she had never worked with metals before, she took lessons from a noted smith one winter to assist in designing and forging an elaborate set of wrought-iron gates to their home.

Daisy began to have what were called "internal abscesses," although it is not known exactly what they were. Her illnesses took her to the Continent for a "cure."

Billow began to make more hunting trips abroad—to Africa, India, and Albania—and to go yachting, without Daisy, which led to her hosting her family members for long stays. Daisy took Mabel to Egypt with her as her companion. They became friends with Mr. and Mrs. Rudyard Kipling.

In 1898 the Spanish American War began. Willie Gordon was made a brigadier general, and Nellie accompanied him to Miami when he took over the command. Arthur and Bill became part of their father's staff.

Daisy joined the cause. The camping conditions of the men in Willie's brigade were deplorable, and many men were dying. Nellie went into action, securing a donated building for a better hospital and helping to nurse the men. One evening the typhoid patients had no milk. After scouring the city and finding no milk for sale, Daisy found a woman who kept a few cows in her yard. She milked the cows herself because the hired hand had gone home for the day!

By the time the Gordon family members returned to Savannah at the close of the war for Mabel's wedding, Daisy's marriage was disintegrating. Billow continued to act as if he were a bachelor, showing little concern for his wife's feelings. Although she did not complain to her family, she wrote her brother Bill in August 1897, ". . . Billow and I are still at odds." Two years later she told Bill, "I see so little of Billow I feel there is no human affection for me." To keep herself distracted, she worked a great deal in organized charities, of which Billow disapproved.

In 1901 Billow went to a facility to cure his heavy drinking, taking along a widow who began to appear with him in public. Daisy ignored the gossip until Billow brought the woman to stay in their home; then she left for Savannah. A year later, when Billow wrote Daisy and asked her agreement for them to live apart, Daisy wrote her consent.

Although Daisy did not want a divorce, Billow demanded one in exchange for a financial settlement. The negotiations lingered for three years. When Daisy learned that Billow's drinking had brought him nearly to the point of death, she stalled the divorce proceedings. Billow died in June 1905; Daisy was now a widow.

Billow left all his money to the other woman; Daisy didn't even own a home. She spent months in legal wrangling to get what was due her. Throughout the entire ordeal, she won the respect of others because of the dignity she maintained. She bought a house in London and entered into the social life there. She spent her winters in Savannah and bought her first car. She was a terrible driver, and locals developed the habit of jumping out of her way. For six years after her husband's death, Daisy traveled as far as Egypt and India. She then began a study of sculpture in Paris.

Daisy, now fifty-one years old, grew closer to her father and spent a great deal of time with him at his farm north of Savannah. Back in London, she met General Sir Robert Baden-Powell, a military hero. They shared common interests: traveling, poetry, sculpting, and creating activities for young people. Both had ancestors who had lived in the American Midwestern wilderness. Baden-Powell had grown up in England, and his mother had taught him much about the out-of-doors. He had taught himself wilderness skills and had taught his soldiers how to track and remember what they saw.

Love of those skills and a desire to teach them to others had led to his organizing the Boy Scouts, which at that time numbered forty thousand members in Great Britain, France, Germany, and the United States.

A friendship developed between Daisy and the general. She wrote this entry in her diary: "[Baden-Powell] believes I might make more out of life, and that he has *ideas* which, if I follow them, will open a more useful sphere of work before me in future." She later wrote: ". . . I told him about . . . the shame I feel when I think of how . . . little I accomplish. . . . A wasted life. He . . . said, 'There are little stars that guide us on, although we do not realize it.'"

Daisy became interested in the Girl Guides group, an off-shoot of the Boy Scouts. She rounded up seven poor local girls in Scotland and started teaching them various skills, even learning how to spin wool so she could teach them. When she returned to London for the winter season, she started two Girl Guides troops there.

Later, Daisy and Robert Baden-Powell found themselves on the same ship when sailing for the United States, he to visit Scout troops. They agreed that Daisy would start the Girl Guides in America.

Daisy wasted no time starting her new venture. She called a cousin, principal of a local girls' school. "Come right over," she said. "I've got something for the girls of Savannah and all America and all the world and we're going to start it tonight!" She held the first official Girl Guides meeting in the United States on March 12, 1912, in Savannah. The organization grew quickly, with inquiries coming from around the nation. Daisy used her deafness to her advantage in recruiting leaders; she would simply pretend not to hear their refusals. Daisy, who had felt inferior to the women in her family because she had had no children, now had many.

Daisy wanted to combine the Girl Guides and the Campfire Girls, but that did not come about. There were already a few Girl Scout troops in the States, so Daisy changed the name Girl Guides to Girl Scouts. She established the headquarters in Washington, D.C., in June 1913. She became known nationally and received many invitations to speak. The friends she had made during her earlier years came to her aid now. Mr. and Mrs. Herbert Hoover gave their support, with Mrs. Hoover serving as the third president of the national organization in 1922. When Hoover became president, Mrs. Hoover used her influence to promote the Girl Scouts.

In 1915 the organization of Girl Scouts was incorporated in the District of Columbia. At its first annual convention, Juliette Low officially became the first president. By early 1916 the Girl Scouts had seven thousand members nationwide. For the first four years, Daisy paid all the administrative expenses, which included her own traveling and lodging expenses; salaries of all staff persons; National Headquarters rent; and patents, uniforms, and handbooks.

Daisy wore her uniform constantly and loved it. In 1919, she represented the American Girl Scouts in London for the first international meeting to connect Girl Guides around the world. Later that year, the Scouts recognized the need for trained professional workers. Daisy realized that her strong personality and style of leadership, which had been helpful in starting the organization, now hurt it. Because she wouldn't listen to others' opinions, she could be difficult to work with. Her hearing problems and her playfulness meant that she disrupted meetings. Further, she was having health problems. Upon her resignation as president in late 1919, she received the title of Founder, and her birthday was designated "Founder's Day." Daisy then spent her time developing scout groups around the nation and the world.

No one knows when Daisy first suspected she had cancer because she kept quiet about it. Possibly it was in 1923. The work of the Girl Scouts was progressing. Leadership training classes had been established in colleges and universities; training camps had been established around the country; and the Brownies had been organized for younger girls. By 1924, 100,000 girls belonged to the Girl Scouts.

Daisy had an operation in Richmond, Virginia, and then secretly left the hospital to speak at a Scout conference. She returned to the hospital and collapsed. In January 1924, while visiting England, her symptoms recurred, but she kept on traveling around the United States and to other countries on Girl Scouts business. At a meeting in England of the International Council of Girl Guides and Girl Scouts, she demanded that the fourth World Camp, scheduled for the summer of 1926, be held in the United States. She responded to objections that many girls could not afford to travel to America by committing the American Girl Scouts to pay the way for one girl from every country.

Daisy further astounded Girl Guide leaders by saying the meeting of four hundred people would take place at Camp Edith Macy in New York State. Jane Rippin, the national director, insisted that the camp—not yet begun—would not be ready. Daisy said, "Jane, if we don't have it next summer, I won't be here. But don't say a word to anyone."

After the conclusion of the World Camp, Daisy collapsed. Near the end of her life, her family sent word to the Girl Scouts headquarters, and Daisy received many flowers and messages. She asked that the most pleasing one, the Girl Scout National Council's telegram, be buried with her. It read: "You are not only the first Girl Scout, you are the best Girl Scout of them all."

Daisy died on January 18, 1927. All the Savannah Girl Scouts lined the steps of the church for her funeral service. Their founder was buried in her uniform with the telegram tucked into her breast pocket.

Daisy had believed that friendship between girls and women across national boundaries could make a vital contribution toward world peace. After her death, friends started the Daisy Low World Friendship Fund, which still provides travel each year for Girl Scouts and Girl Guides members between the United States and other countries.

In 1954 the Scouts bought the Gordon house in Savannah and made it into a museum to which Girl Scouts make pilgrimages each year.

As of September 2000, 2,404,471 girls and 802,687 adults were active in Girl Scouts in the United States. One hundred and forty countries belong to the Worldwide Association of Girl Guides and Girl Scouts. Daisy was right when she said, "I've got something for the girls of Savannah and all America and all the world!"

MARTHA McCHESNEY BERRY

1866–1942

Miracle Lady of the Mountains

$\mathcal{A}$s a child Martha Berry rode with her father, Thomas Berry, into the mountains north of Rome, Georgia, as Captain Berry made his regular visits to the homes of the men who had served in his Civil War infantry company. Martha had been born in 1866, a year after the war's end.

Before Captain Berry left for the war in 1861, he did something that few other Southern businessmen did: He paid his debts owed to Northerners. During his three-year absence, his wife, Frances, oversaw their cotton plantation and served as the plantation physician.

In November 1864 Union soldiers swept through Georgia, stealing food, burning buildings, and killing animals they couldn't eat or use. After they set fire to the Berry farm, sparks from smoldering outbuildings blew onto Oak Hill, the family's large home, but Frances Berry and the slaves saved the house.

When Captain Berry returned from the war, his earlier acts of integrity enabled him to borrow $50,000 from northern businessmen. He reestablished his businesses of raising cotton, running a cotton brokerage, and operating a cotton manufactory.

Martha Berry

The men who had made up his infantry found it hard to make a living in the war-ravaged Georgia mountains, so Thomas Berry continued to help them. But, he told Martha, "I have to help them in a way that doesn't hurt their dignity," so he didn't give them charity money. He would instead give them seed to plant, for example.

Martha was shocked at the poverty in which the mountain people lived. She had no way of knowing that her sensibilities were being touched in a way that would determine her life's work.

In addition to her parents' guidance, Martha came under the influence of "Aunt" Martha, a slave—later a free person—who practically ran the Berry home. If a child behaved rudely, she would scold her by saying, "A Berry don' ack lak dat." Another influence on Martha was the Berry children's governess. Georgia had few schools at that time, so Thomas Berry employed Miss Ida McCullough to teach the children in a log cabin in a pine grove.

The Berry girls were expected to grow up to be traditional Southern belles, which required going away to a finishing school. Martha's older sister Jennie rushed to fulfil that role, but Martha didn't want to leave home. Her father sent her to a school in Baltimore, but Martha felt so uncomfortable there that she stayed only at her father's insistence. She happily returned home when her father became ill. She served as her father's companion and, in spite of a lifelong shyness, made trips into the mountains on her father's behalf.

After five years of illness, Captain Berry told Martha that he feared he would not live much longer. "I am going to will to you the tract of land across the road," he told her. "Land and trees . . . they'll never lose their worth. Look after them and they'll support you."

Captain Berry encouraged his daughter, with her lovely, rounded figure, black hair, and beautiful complexion, to spend more time with suitors. No man pleased her until a distant cousin also named Berry came to visit. Recognizing his daughter's interest in the man, Captain Berry offered him a job in his factory to aid the romance. The two became engaged, but Thomas Berry's death led Martha to put off the marriage, and the cousin returned home.

Martha visited the mountains of northern Alabama with a friend named Emma. They employed a young mountain man as their guide. Emma and the young man later married, even though he could neither read nor write. When Martha visited the couple later, she saw that Emma had aged tremendously in only a little time. It distressed her to learn that Emma's husband had given up his intentions of getting an education. This visit made a deep impression on Martha, strengthening her wish to help give mountain people an education.

Back home, Martha cleaned the Berry schoolhouse to make a private reading room. One Sunday afternoon, as she sat there reading her Bible, some mountain children appeared at the window. Martha invited them in, gave them apples to eat, and told them Bible stories. Her inquiries revealed that the children had no school or church; the roof of their community's building had caved in. She invited them to return to her schoolhouse the next Sunday and to bring others with them.

They did, and over time adults began to come, too. The crowds grew to forty each Sunday, and some people were walking eight miles each way to attend Martha's homemade church and school services. Martha rode her horse into the mountains to see the tumbledown church in the Possum Trot community at the foot of Lavendar Mountain. She organized a workday to renovate the building, promising food only to those who worked. She thus succeeded in bossing men, something seldom tolerated by mountain folk. She earned the name "Sunday Lady" by going to the church weekly to tell Bible stories. She became a circuit rider, visiting three other churches the people had spruced up. To lighten her load, her sister Frances took over the work at some of the locations.

Martha's suitor came from Virginia to press her again regarding marriage. When she said she could not leave her work, he left again. Though she grieved for a time, she said, "Like a nun, I have married an ideal."

Martha visited the mountain people on weekdays and taught children poems and sayings. These smart children needed more formal education, she recognized. She decided to open a day school on the property her father had left her.

For one hundred dollars and help from hired workmen and volunteer mountain boys, she had a one-room building constructed. Planks became benches for students, crates became desks, and a wooden packing case provided her a desk.

The school opened on January 13, 1902, with five students and two teachers, Martha and Frances.

On some days bad roads and weather prevented the children from attending, and at spring planting time—after five months of school—the children had to stay at home to help. Because parents needed their children's help on the farm, they hesitated to send them back for the new school term. The children who did return had usually forgotten what they had been taught.

The number of students grew in spite of the obstacles. To accommodate the overflow, Martha started branch schools in the church buildings formerly used for Sunday schools. She persuaded friends to teach classes there. When she wrote to Elizabeth Brewster, a college graduate, asking her to come teach for a small salary, Miss Brewster came on the next train.

Martha saw that the older boys needed to stay in a setting where they could learn constantly, instead of returning home each day. She decided she would persuade the parents to release the boys from work by offering to teach them courses that would relate to their environments. That plan would require money, however, and the boys would need somewhere to live near the school. She took the deed to her father's land to the bank and deeded the land to the children of the Appalachian Mountains.

Martha sought the help of a retired architect to build a dormitory. To furnish it, she took furniture from her own home and called on church members in Rome to donate items. She named the school the Boys Industrial School and the dormitory Brewster Hall. She and Elizabeth Brewster moved into the building. Martha went to the chairman of the county school board for help hiring more teachers.

Martha then took on the monumental task of persuading parents to allow their sons to attend. Students would spend part of each day working on the farm, she told the parents. She thus became one of the first educators in the United States to set up a work-study plan. By 1912 Georgia had established eleven district agricultural and mechanical schools patterned after hers, and other states followed suit.

Martha had the four fundamentals she considered basic to human happiness emblazoned in quarters on the school shield: the Bible for prayer, the lamp for learning, the plow for labor, and the cabin for simplicity.

The first Saturday after the boys moved in, Martha told them they had to wash their own clothes. "No'm," the boys protested. "Men don' wash clothes. That's woman's work." Martha plunged her hands into the washtubs, and then the boys offered to take over the task.

Over the years, Martha pitched in to meet any need that arose. When the first cook quit, she and Elizabeth Brewster took over the job of satisfying the appetites of the hungry students.

In May 1904 one boy was ready to graduate, so Martha planned a commencement. Always one to plan big, she invited the Honorable Hoke Smith, former secretary of the interior under President Grover Cleveland and the man predicted to be Georgia's next governor. Smith tried to beg out of the invitation later due to fatigue, but Martha wouldn't let him off the hook. He couldn't believe it when he found out there was only one person in the graduating class!

Smith spent the night in the dormitory, and he got little sleep due to the boys' noise. He gave Martha a generous check "if you promise to build a good, solid dormitory." She promised and told him it would be called the Hoke Smith Cottage.

The next year students from neighboring states came to attend the school, and many brought livestock to pay their tuition. Because she had so little actual money coming in, Martha's need for funds grew to an alarming level. She tried to hide this fact from the boys, but one night at evening prayers, one boy prayed, "Lord, Miss Berry told us we ought not to ask You to send things, but jes' let You know we'll do what we kin if You'll show the way. . . . I'm wonderin', Lord, whether You ain't showin' the way right now. I read in the paper about some New York people givin' money to schools. Dear God, give Miss Berry strength to get up there and tell them folks how much we need things. Amen."

That prayer sparked an idea in Martha's mind. In spite of her shyness, she took a train to New York in November 1904. She used the new invention, the telephone, to call some of her friends from finishing school. She was invited to lunch with some of her old friends, now wives of wealthy men. To her disappointment, they responded coolly to her appeals for funds. One friend referred her to a church for help.

Martha spoke at the church, and the members did offer some help. The pastor referred her to one of the richest men in the city. When she went to his office and told him about the school, he asked, "And what do you get out of this, Miss Berry?"

"I'm afraid I don't understand the question," Martha said.

"What is your salary? What is your pay for all this work?"

After a pause, Martha said, "I get everything out of it—all the thrill of watching these neglected, illiterate boys turn into clear-thinking, educated young men who will return to their communities and change them!"

The man gave her a check and promised an annual donation. She didn't look at the check until she was ready to board a streetcar. The check was for $500, enough for ten full scholarships!

In her excitement, she walked back to the boardinghouse in the snow without galoshes. The next day she had pneumonia. By the time she had recovered sufficiently to take the train home, she had raised $1,800—a fortune to her.

That spring, the schoolhouse burned down. The school held graduation exercises in a borrowed tent. After a new building was built, Martha had the architect design a wide Gate of Opportunity at the campus entrance.

The need for money, always desperate, became greater after the fire. Martha returned to New York and received $10,000 from an eccentric man who put her to an unusual test: He would give the money only if she cared enough about the school to come to see him at midnight. She passed the test and received the money, the largest amount donated in the history of the school.

On the school's farm the boys raised cows, which supplied milk and dairy products for dormitory residents and for outside sales; they grew corn, hay, tomatoes, and peaches, and they raised hogs and goats. Martha decreed that all boys would wear a uniform—blue denim shirts and overalls with matching jackets—so poorer boys wouldn't feel ashamed of their clothing.

A nationwide economic panic in 1907 caused even greater pressure for Martha to raise money for the school. She worked so hard that she went to bed with a heavy cold. A telephone call from the governor awakened her. "I have just learned that Andrew Carnegie is going through Atlanta this evening on his way north. I would like for you to be in the receiving line at the reception," he said.

"Of course, I'll come," replied Martha.

Martha put a ten-year-old blue gown and a long ostrich-feather-trimmed cape into a bag and caught the train to Atlanta. Mr. Carnegie gave her no time to talk during the reception, so Martha boarded his departing train, hoping to get his attention. He went to bed before Martha could speak to one of his aides, who suggested that Martha stay and eat breakfast with him.

Martha made her appeal to the benefactor in her unsuitable attire at breakfast, but Mr. Carnegie only told her to come to see him in New York. She returned to Atlanta by train from Washington, D.C., still in her evening garb. She spent the next week in the hospital.

Martha's next important contact was with President Theodore Roosevelt. A writer who had visited Martha had passed on to the president word about the school and advised Martha to visit Roosevelt. Martha sent him a letter, and the president responded to Martha's note by inviting her to Washington. She wore a plain brown coat and skirt and sat beside Roosevelt on a horsehair coach as she showed him an album of photographs and told him about the school. The president responded enthusiastically to Martha's story and invited her to have dinner with him and his wife that evening. Martha's sister Frances had thrown away the blue gown and ostrich cape and bought her an elegant evening gown for such occasions. Martha made many important contacts at that dinner.

She continued on to New York, where her goal was to see Andrew Carnegie. The philanthropist continued to rebuff her efforts for a meeting. In her typical persistent manner, she went to his room and wrote a note on a card for the butler to take to him. Carnegie called Martha in to talk while he was posing for a portrait. He asked her to fill out a lengthy form giving facts about the school.

Martha called the school, collected the data requested on the form, and received from Carnegie a check for $50,000 with the condition that she raise an equal amount from other sources. She continued to raise funds for two weeks, then Carnegie called to ask how she was doing. She had only $7,000, so he invited her to join him for tea with a wealthy woman who had already declined to give to the school. During the meeting, Carnegie virtually blackmailed the woman by hinting that if she did not help the school, he would not help her with a project of her own. The woman offered a pledge of $25,000.

Back home, Martha still had to raise $18,000. She contacted a wealthy Atlantan, Mrs. Frank Inman, who had shown an earlier interest in the school. Mrs. Inman started a group called Berry Circle to raise money for the school; soon other circles developed around the state. Martha raised the required $50,000.

Martha was distressed when she had to turn down female applicants to the school, so in 1908, she decided to open a girls' boarding school. One girl walked to the Berry school with her brother, promising to "he'p with the plowin' an' the dairyin,' too." Martha wanted poor girls to learn how to be better homemakers and crafters so they could sell mountain crafts for money.

The Board of Trustees and the highlanders themselves vetoed Martha's idea to educate girls, to put both sexes together, or to duplicate expenses by having a separate school for girls, but Martha went ahead with her plan. One evening, while walking up a narrow mountain path she came upon a large deserted cabin a mile from the boys' school. "This will be the first building of the Girls' School," she decided instantly, "and around it we will build other cottages like it."

She set Thanksgiving as opening day, enlisting the aid of the boys to repair the cabin, to build new buildings, and to invite girls. She visited Rome churches to get furnishings and supplies. The school opened with twenty-five girls, who made their own uniforms on sewing machines that the Singer Company had donated. By the time the Board of Trustees found out what was happening, it was too late for them to intervene.

Like the boys, the girls spent half their days in classes and half working—gardening, housekeeping, spinning, and weaving. Martha bought a herd of Angora goats; the boys sheared the wool, then the girls washed it, carded it, and spun it. They sold their products to raise money for the school.

The girls took on the responsibility of cooking for guests, and Theodore Roosevelt was one of their first. He arrived at the end of a six-week drought. It poured rain the afternoon of his arrival, and he rolled up his pants legs and drove himself from the train station to the campus on an oxcart.

Roosevelt spoke to the students, then he spent the night in a log guest cabin that Martha then named the "Roosevelt Cabin." In his speech, he said that the ideal citizen is "a lifter, not a leaner." Martha adopted that phrase as the school's slogan, then later changed it to "Not to be ministered unto, but to minister."

Martha could never rest. She next envisioned having three divisions of the school, adding a boarding grammar school. She proceeded with her dream rather than heeding the protests of the Board of Trustees. Her dream included buying additional land for expansion and building a bigger chapel. The tiny log cabin church no longer served the school's needs. "More and more Berry boys are marrying Berry girls," she said, "and I want to have a beautiful place for their weddings."

She even decided where to place the chapel: in a grove of trees on land she did not yet own! To further complicate the situation, she heard that the owner planned to sell the property for use as a country club. "Over my dead body!" Martha exclaimed and headed out to plead with the owner to give her three months to find the money. He agreed, and she found the required $10,000 in New York only hours before the deadline.

That fund-raising trip to New York wore her out so much that her doctor ordered her to take a complete rest. Her sisters and brothers pooled their finances to buy a roundtrip steamship ticket for her to Rome, Italy. She went to visit her sister Jennie, who had married and lived there. She talked to other passengers about Berry school and came away with more financial donations.

While Martha was in Europe, World War I started, and Americans were requested to come home. Back in Georgia, she bade tearful goodbyes to Berry boys who went overseas after the United States entered the war. Some of those young men did not return.

Martha never took a rest from fund-raising. One day at age fifty-seven she read in an Atlanta newspaper that Mr. and Mrs. Henry Ford would be visiting in Alabama. Mr. Ford had never responded to her appeals for money, and Martha knew that he did not give to schools or most charitable efforts to help the poor or handicapped. "If I can just get him to Berry, he'll see that it is different," she said.

Off she went to the town where the Fords were staying. She had met Mrs. Ford before, so she sent her a note asking if they could meet again. Mrs. Ford invited Martha to visit her and her husband that evening. As Martha always had done, she did research on Mr. Ford so she could mention topics that would touch his heart. She apparently succeeded, because he said, "I think I'd like to see the school for myself."

The three arrived at Berry at dinnertime, and the Fords enjoyed the corn chowder, beaten biscuits, herb-cured ham, and yams the students served. Mr. Ford marveled that the students had grown the items as well as cooked them. A tour through the kitchen led Mrs. Ford to comment on the outdated equipment.

The Fords later donated money to build a girls' dormitory and a dining hall with a kitchen. Ford's architect designed lavish buildings that were too complicated for the boys, who had built the earlier buildings, to construct themselves. Ford sent Italian stone-cutters to build the Gothic buildings. When the Fords visited later, Henry offered to give tractors so the boys could stop plowing with mules. When he learned that the girls made dresses from flour sacks, he offered to supply all the flour Berry needed.

The Fords visited the school annually from then on, and Henry Ford donated two more buildings. That gave Martha the confidence to share with her benefactors her dream of having a quadrangle surrounded by four Gothic buildings. Ford immediately agreed to spend the millions of dollars that would be required. Martha could remember when she considered a $500 gift a generous donation.

Unfortunately, the Fords' gifts created a problem for the school and for Martha. The extra dormitories drew more students, which called for more teachers, additional food, and other supplies. The fact that the Fords did not provide any funds for maintenance of the new buildings added to the problems. Further, the grand buildings gave the public the idea that Berry no longer needed financial help. Martha noted, "They think we're rich, and I haven't the slightest idea where we'll get the money to pay teachers' salaries next month!"

Martha began to receive national recognition for her work. She went to Washington to receive the Theodore Roosevelt Medal of Distinguished Service to her country from President Calvin Coolidge, and she received honorary degrees from a dozen universities. Celebrations of Berry's twenty-fifth anniversary took place during 1927. During that year, Martha announced that Berry would open a junior college for both men and women in the fall with plans to increase it to a senior college.

Even though some benefactors offered to pay to have their students attend, Martha continued to take only students who could not afford to go elsewhere. Berry's annual endowment grew to $100,000, and products and crops the students sold brought in an equal amount. Even so, Martha also had to raise that much each year to keep the school afloat.

The Depression brought severe financial problems for the school. People withdrew pledges, and checks bounced. Martha saw people practically begging to earn a living. Seeing the abundant crops and herds on campus, she devised a plan to let people live on campus in tents and work to earn a living. To accommodate the newcomers, new crops were planted, an addition was built onto the cannery, new buildings were built, and a pine forest was planted. The campus supported several people during those trying years.

The school's finances slumped to a desperate state. Martha asked staff and faculty members to take cuts in their already low salaries. When it looked as if the school might close, an eccentric woman gave the amount needed to pull the school out of its slump in mid-1933. In total, Martha probably raised $25 million for the school over the years.

By the time Martha turned seventy-three, her health was failing. Everyone agreed that she needed a rest, so she went to London, where friends arranged to have her presented to the queen. She balked at the idea of purchasing a new gown for the event, saying the money could be spent for her students. When she realized she could wear the new dress when she gave away students at their weddings, she finally agreed to shop for the gown.

Unfortunately, Martha's health did not improve. High blood pressure and heart disease took her to an Atlanta hospital for months. Although she returned home, she reentered the hospital just before her seventy-fifth birthday. On February 27, 1942, the bell in the Berry chapel tower tolled seventy-five strokes. That afternoon, a black hearse drove through the Gate of Opportunity and toward the old log cabin chapel. The boys and girls lined the road as they always did to receive guests. The students sang a hymn, one of Martha's favorites. They then laid her to rest on the college campus.

Today more than 1,100 undergraduate and graduate students attend Berry College on its campus of 28,000 acres, the largest in the world. In addition, children attend a kindergarten and an elementary school on the grounds. It all started in a log cabin on a Sunday afternoon with Bible stories for poor mountain children.

LUGENIA
BURNS HOPE
1872–1947

Social Activist

$\mathcal{L}$ugenia Burns Hope, who became one of the most effective African-American social reformers in the South, spoke boldly for a black woman in the 1920s. "It is difficult for me to understand why my white sisters so strenuously object to this honest expression of colored women as put forth in the discarded preamble," she said. She was referring to the white women's hesitation to support federal antilynching legislation. "After all," she continued, "when we yield to public opinion and make ourselves say only what we think the public can stand, is there not a danger that we may find ourselves with our larger view conceding what those with the narrow view demand?" Thus Mrs. Hope forced the white women belonging to her antilynching organization to face their own racial beliefs and fears.

Lugenia Burns was born on February 19, 1872, in St. Louis, Missouri, the youngest child of Ferdinand and Louisa M. Bertha Burns. She was called "Genie" by her family. Lugenia's paternal grandfather, William Burns—a white man who was a wealthy plow manufacturer—had been Mississippi's secretary of state during the

Lugenia Burns Hope

1850s. Lugenia's grandmother was an African American. The couple lived openly with their five children as an interracial family in Nachez; interracial marriages were illegal at the time. Lugenia's maternal grandfather, of French descent, had migrated to Mississippi from Canada.

The date when Lugenia's parents married is not certain, but by 1880 they had seven children. Her father's sudden death led her mother to relocate to Chicago during the premigration period of the late 1800s, specifically to give Genie superior educational opportunities. The Burnses found themselves living among segregationists in a city that had once been an Underground Railroad station. Now many whites feared the loss of their jobs to blacks and urged passage of Jim Crow laws. In spite of that hostile climate, the black community had put down deep roots in Chicago and had made important political gains by 1885. The so-called "Black Belt" had its own medical, business, and social establishments.

Genie was able to go to school, aided by her older brothers who supported the family. She even took classes at the Art Institute of Chicago. These classes would bear fruit later when she taught sculpture classes in her attic to college students and arts and crafts to underprivileged children in Atlanta.

When Genie was a teenager, her brothers lost their employment, and she had to drop out of school. She went to work as a bookkeeper for a printing company and as a dressmaker. After that period, she became the first black secretary to the board of directors of Kings Daughters, a Chicago charitable organization. In that capacity she worked with teenage working girls, an experience that also bore fruit in Genie's later years in Atlanta. When a white woman offered Genie the position of managing a new business, she continued working with the girls in the evenings. She would later describe these years as a "rich and thrilling experience."

By working and supporting her family, Genie grew more and more independent. Because she knew she could take care of herself, she examined suitors carefully to ensure they would be able to provide adequately for a family. She did not feel the need to marry for economic security, as did many women of her generation. She also wanted to marry a man who would recognize her as an economic equal in the marriage. Furthermore, she was a pretty young woman who did not have trouble attracting men.

Lugenia Burns found a man who met her qualifications on August 21, 1893, at a dance held for blacks in connection with the World's Columbian Exposition held in Chicago. His name was John Hope, a theology student at Brown University in Providence, Rhode Island. John had been born in Augusta, Georgia, in 1868, the son of a mixed-race mother and a Scottish father. Although he had fair skin, blue eyes, and blond hair, he identified with blacks. At first, he did not overly impress Lugenia, and the "steady gaze from his blue eyes made her quite uncomfortable."

John, who had to work his way through college, had had little time for romance or money to spend on a young woman. No previous female had affected him the way Lugenia did. In *The Story of John Hope*, Ridgely Torrence wrote: ". . . he met a young woman whose image seized upon his mind and emotions in a way that astonished the hitherto unsusceptible John Hope." What John remembered was "the undeniably pretty face and sun-rich coloring of the girl he had met [at the dance]."

They met a second time and soon discovered together that Lugenia's vivaciousness complemented John's reserved nature, a trait that people attributed to his Scottish heritage. On their third meeting, John treated Lugenia to an ice cream soda. That outlay of expense left him with only $1.50 in his pocket. They dated until John returned to his classes, and a subsequent exchange of letters drew them close.

John wrote Lugenia of his dream of returning to his native South after graduation in 1894. A faculty committee had pronounced his plans foolish and offered him a position as a reporter for a Providence newspaper. His heart won out, though, and John started teaching at Roger Williams University, a black school in Nashville, Tennessee. Though he was drawn to the ministry, John had decided to try the teaching profession. For several summers, he studied in Chicago in order to be near Lugenia. Their long courtship, punctuated by John's proposals, tried his patience.

Lugenia, now twenty-four years old, felt caught between her obligation to take care of her then-deaf mother and her desire to marry John. The guilt she felt toward her mother led to health problems. To complicate the situation further, four wealthy men proposed to her. Her family urged her to accept one of them rather than marry poor John Hope who would take her back to the racist South. When John, whom Lugenia called Jack, wrote that he had "withdrawn himself from other women and now was exclusively hers," she accepted his proposal of marriage.

John gave his fiancée his father's small heirloom ring, and she began to lay down conditions for their marriage. First, she would run the household. When John spoke of her "work" after the marriage as her being interested in his affairs, she began to doubt if she had chosen the right man. Lugenia intended to continue doing community work as she had done in Chicago after they were married.

They resolved their differences, and Lugenia, twenty-six, married John, twenty-nine, in December 1897. They moved into the boys' dorm at the Nashville school, and Lugenia started teaching a class in physical education.

John's invitation to teach at Atlanta Baptist College, a school that had been started to educate freed slaves, led them back to his beloved Georgia in the fall of 1898. Again the couple lived in the school dormitory, Graves Hall. The college had a white president, and black students were drawn to the Hopes for everything from advice to help getting a job or a dose of castor oil. The couple did not keep precise office hours, but they were available at all times in their second-floor room.

John taught Greek and Latin and started a football program. Lugenia helped support the football team, even making pennants by hand for students to wave at games.

Lugenia could not have chosen a better setting for her love of social work. Spelman, Atlanta Baptist, and Clark Colleges exchanged faculties and shared classrooms—and were located in the center of a slum area. The first morning she awakened in Atlanta, Lugenia looked out her bedroom window. In "Social Work Among Atlanta Negroes," Louise D. Shivery described what she saw:

> The West Side was a neglected section of the city. Fair Street was a slum, full of holes, mud, and debris. Areas named "Beaver's Slide," White's Alley, Peters Street and Roach Street terrified even children because of fights, brawls, gambling, and killings that were all too frequent occurrences. Beckwith Street . . . was full of hillocks and holes, mud and rocks, with no pavements. The city used it as a dump for rubbish. As late as 1914 automobiles and wagons could not go through. Chestnut Street, flanking this section, was partly developed first by whites, later by graduates of Atlanta University, Spelman, and Morehouse, who built homes on the street to live near the colleges. But there were no water mains, and residents had to appeal to the City Council to stop the burning of garbage in the area because of the resultant stench and smoke. Behind Atlanta University on the

north was a similar section . . . where slums, dumps, hovels, crime, and want prevailed. Directly behind this section, going north, was another section known as "Lightning" where the city permitted houses of ill repute. On the other side of Atlanta, going south, was . . . a Negro settlement in which many Negroes owned small pieces of unimproved property, and where the same neglect as to lights, water, sewerage, pavements, and housing prevailed.

Beaver Slide, the section nearest Lugenia's room, had flourished during the Civil War when soldiers spent their money there on saloons and prostitutes. The area then became an outlaw community where criminals could hide, getting its name when a criminal succeeded in hiding from the law there.

Although Lugenia was an outsider and still very young, John Hope later said she was "among the first (if not the very first) to do volunteer social work in Atlanta and to organize the city for social work on a volunteer basis."

The children of the neighborhood had caught Lugenia's attention as soon as she had arrived in Atlanta. Lugenia focused on Battle Alley, hoping to open day care centers in the neighborhood. She gathered a small group of women around her. They called themselves the Neighborhood Union and chose "And Thy Neighbor as Thyself" as their motto. They bravely walked through Battle Alley, or Low's Alley, the entrance to the dangerous neighborhood. It was typical for them to see a dead man, a fact that police ignored. Each woman chose a different alley as her charge. The Neighborhood Union members approached local female residents with respect and gradually overcame the locals' original resistance to their presence. They began to offer the women help to raise their children and improve their dismal lots in life.

Lugenia attended a conference on "The Welfare of the Negro Child." She later served on a board and agreed to chair a committee to develop free kindergartens for children who were left home alone while their mothers went to work. The Gate City Free Kindergarten Association grew out of that work in 1904.

Alonzo Herndon, a black Atlanta millionaire, gave the new association a large building and paid a teacher's salary for several years. The kindergarten program expanded to become a day-care center.

Although John and Lugenia kept busy with their tasks, they had the opportunity to take a vacation in the spring of 1900 when John participated in a convention in Detroit. They visited Niagara Falls on their way back home. When they returned to Atlanta, they rented a cottage in nearby Lithia Springs. Lugenia stayed at home while John traveled.

Lugenia's interest in the needs of local mothers grew when she became the mother of a son, Edward, on August 28, 1901. John joked with a friend, "A little Hope is better than no Hope at all." John had a great fear of being in debt, so rather than buying a house for his family, the Hopes moved to larger quarters on the ground floor of Graves Hall.

At that time, John received a tempting offer to teach theology at Virginia Union University in Richmond, Virginia. The move would include a raise, something a family man could not ignore. After consideration, though, John followed his heart and stayed in Atlanta, earning $1,500 a year for many years. Lugenia would live on the college campus for a total of thirty-nine years.

In June 1906 John was inaugurated as president of Atlanta Baptist, becoming the first black president of a Baptist college. The family moved into the designated president's house. It was in that home that Lugenia taught sculpture in the attic and turned a closet into a darkroom where she developed and printed her own negatives. Atlanta Baptist College later changed its name to Morehouse College, and John remained president until 1929.

As Edward grew, Lugenia learned that there was no playground or park where she could take her black child. An angry Lugenia rallied other college mothers, who secured space on the college campus for a playground. The work the women did became the nucleus of other community organizations.

All of the faculty, staff, and students helped raise Edward, who grew up unaware of the racial climate of his world. Edward became especially fascinated by the power plant where W. T. Courtney, the superintendent of buildings and grounds at Spelman College, satisfied the boy's curiosity about the big engine and the huge wheel. Edward early told his parents he wanted to be an engineer when he grew up. John feared that Edward's race might block his achieving that ambition, but Edward's experiences while growing up later brought him credits from the Massachusetts Institute of Technology, and he eventually did become an engineer.

In the summer of 1906, two events took place that had serious implications for race relations in Atlanta. First, John was the only college president, black or white, to attend the Niagara Movement meeting in Harper's Ferry, West Virginia. Founded by W. E. B. DuBois, Monroe Trotter, Mary Burnett Talbert, and several others, the movement had sprouted from a secret meeting of prominent blacks held in Buffalo, New York, the previous year. In 1906 the group met openly to speak boldly of the needs of blacks to receive racial justice. Attending the event could have threatened John's career and even his life. The Niagara Movement led to the creation of the National Association for the Advancement of Colored People (NAACP).

Second, about the time of John's return, racial tension that had been smoldering for some time in Atlanta erupted. A race riot broke out on September 22. Whites attacked streetcars and beat innocent blacks on the streets and in shops. Blacks fled to the college campuses for refuge. The riot lasted three days, leaving a great deal of physical destruction and injuring and killing many black citizens.

The faculty and students of Atlanta Baptist College were devastated emotionally, and the campus had suffered physical damage. John had to decide whether or not to open for the new semester. He went ahead with the opening, bringing admiration from college personnel.

The arrival of the Hopes' second son, John Hope II, on Christmas Day, 1909, brought disappointment for John, who had wanted a daughter, but further inspiration for Lugenia, who hoped to improve conditions for black children in Atlanta.

Lugenia believed in discipline for her children but used physical punishment only when humor and lectures failed. Both John and Lugenia's work took them on frequent trips, but they tried not to be away at the same time, and the boys did not feel neglected. John II, in particular, became the pet of the Morehouse College students, so much so that Lugenia placed a sign around his neck reading, "Please do not feed this animal." Lugenia expected her children to contribute to their family life, and Edward would go with his mother to the millinery class she taught to Spelman students and work the connecting rod on his mother's foot-operated sewing machine.

Since black guests had trouble finding lodging in the city, Lugenia found herself acting as a hotel proprietor. Edward called their home a sort of "defacto glorified guest house." White and foreign guests also stayed in their home. Lugenia managed to provide comfort for all, even with a limited budget. Students, family members, and hired help worked in the home, supplementing Lugenia's efforts.

Lugenia's interest in the arts led her to become a charter member of the Inquirers, a social and literary club formed in February 1909. The club met weekly to have fellowship and to discuss current events and Shakespeare.

John remarked about how caring Lugenia was to others. In 1912 he wrote her from the *Lusitania:* "You do things so naturally, you love and sacrifice so 'easily' that you are unusual. I believe it must be that quality in you which makes the Neighborhood Union people believe in you."

In 1917 Morehouse College observed its fiftieth anniversary. The school had become recognized as a center of racial equality and community life in Atlanta. In that same year, the United States entered World War I. Lugenia stayed home while John went to France for nine months as a YMCA representative to work with black troops. She gave her services to the YWCA, managing the first black hostess house at Camp Upton and training black women as hostess house secretaries.

Lugenia offered classes in social work through the Neighborhood Union in 1918. These efforts led to the organization of the Social Service Institute at Morehouse College. Her three-day workshop, which provided lectures on childcare and problems with adolescents and emphasized social service, grew into the Atlanta School of Social Work. Lugenia supervised students as they worked in the field. She believed that her major responsibility was to help students develop a sensitivity toward the needs of the black community.

In 1923 Lugenia helped found the Morehouse Auxiliary for staff and faculty wives to develop campus social life and raise money to provide student scholarships and to build the school's first gymnasium.

She continued to support her husband's activities heartily. In 1929, John wrote his appreciation for her efforts:

I wonder how it would have been if I had never met you. I am absolutely sure that I should never have had the success that I have had or risen to positions that have come to me. I bow down to you, my dear little wife, in reverence and love for what you are to me. I want you to know, too, that I am not changed or puffed . . . about anything that has come to me. I want you to share it all with me—the honor and the money.

In addition to her support of her husband, Lugenia continued to take an active interest in social reform. She tried to do so much, however, that the work began to demand too much of her time. This did not make John happy. Shortly before he left Europe to return home from one of his trips, he wrote his wife:

My stay is reaching its close. Eight days more and I shall be on the sea coming home [,] coming to you. How I dream of you all day long as I move about from place to place! Yet when I return you will be so busy that you will have no time to listen to me. Your work as mine takes me from you. You blame me, yet you are too busy for small talk. However, we have been a long time apart and "you" must be more with me.

In an article on Lugenia Burns Hope, Jacqueline Rouse wrote:

. . . one wonders if she needed to be constantly on the move. We can only speculate about how their lengthy absences affected their marriage. Did Lugenia perhaps need new challenges and tasks in order to avoid feelings of loneliness and stagnation? John's letters to her while she was away suggest that her constant activity resulted from her inability to relax and enjoy past accomplishments. He warned her not to overextend herself.

By the spring of 1928, Edward had received his master's degree in hydroelectric engineering from the Massachusetts Institute of Technology. His father's fears had come to pass; because of his race, Edward could not get the job he desired. In Jerusalem, John met an American man who lived in Brazil. Through that man's contacts, Edward spent the next three years in Brazil doing the work he loved.

In 1929 John became president of the Atlanta University Alliance with the mandate to merge Morehouse, Spelman, and Clark Colleges into the first black university in the South. John also kept his position as president of Morehouse until 1931. In 1932, the Hope family moved into the new home for the university president.

Lugenia's community work continued to claim much of her interest and time. In 1933, the Neighborhood Union honored her at a banquet at the time of its twenty-fifth anniversary. Two years later, she resigned her office on the local level but continued to serve at the national level.

Her interests led to other involvements, such as being an officer in the local branch of the NAACP and taking part in the founding session of the National Council of Negro Women. After the war, she helped develop the "Negro branch" of the YWCA; those efforts led to a black woman being appointed to the YWCA's southern field staff for the first time. She also worked against discrimination through church and community groups, an antilynching organization, and the NAACP.

She helped improve education for black students in Atlanta, campaigning for improved schools and increased salaries for teachers. One of her highest achievements was helping develop Booker T. Washington High School, Atlanta's first black high school.

After their sons were grown, Lugenia and John traveled together some, but eventually the couple started to grow apart. John began to travel alone. He was having health problems, and his physician thought getting away from Atlanta would help. John took his secretary (at his family's urging), but not Lugenia, on one of those recovery trips. In 1933 John lived in a hospital on the Spelman College campus for a period after being ill, separated from his wife. Meanwhile, Lugenia supervised the design and construction of a home in north Georgia while continuing her social work.

Although John wrote passionate letters to his wife when he traveled, she heard rumors that he was having affairs with other women, especially with white women. As Lugenia worked with her husband's biographer, Ridgely Torrence, she said: "Some white women were aggressive. But he paid no attention to that. He was a [southern gentleman] and treated all women with the greatest respect. . . . Don't let the few stories that you may hear color the life of the man—because the book would be FALSE."

After a busy day on June 15, 1933, John had a serious heart attack. He was so ill that he and Lugenia could not attend their son John's wedding in July. John Hope recuperated and continued his busy life until he passed away on February 20, 1936.

After her husband's death, Lugenia spent more time with her family. Her grandchildren remember her as being playful. While visiting John II in Nashville, Lugenia died on August 14, 1947. She had requested earlier that her body be cremated and that her funeral service be held at John's home. In November, Morehouse College held a memorial service for her. Again at Lugenia's request, her ashes were scattered over the Morehouse campus from the tower of Graves Hall, "the place she loved most in the entire world."

Lugenia Hope had made a distinct difference in her world. As Jacqueline Rouse wrote:

> Part of her appeal was her radical, undaunting activism; the other was her genuine love and concern for all children and her willingness to struggle to improve their lives. However, her radical style of activism made her far more outspoken than her peers, more demanding, and less willing to compromise on the issues of racial justice and gender equality. She was more accusatory, and more direct, in interracial meetings than most of her colleagues. . . . Her peers praised her courage, her frankness, and the forthright manner in which she exposed deceit, prejudice, and injustice . . . because of Hope the African-American women's agenda was always clear, its priorities always visible. Without question, Hope's work was instrumental in improving the lives of African-American Atlantans during the early years of the twentieth century.

LEILA
ROSS WILBURN
1885–1967

Pioneer Architect

*I*n the Sunday morning edition of the August 24, 1924, *Atlanta Journal,* Frank Daniel opened his article, "Atlanta Women Have Man-Size Jobs," with this sentence: "In Atlanta you can have your home planned by a woman architect." Such a statement was unusual for the time, but it was true. The article celebrated the achievements of Leila Ross Wilburn, Atlanta's first female architect and a fascinating and prolific domestic designer.

Daniel's article included the results of the Southern Woman's Educational Alliance survey which concluded that "women are capable of doing just about anything they make up their minds to do." Other paragraphs described how Leila had established her own office and developed a prosperous business designing homes. A picture accompanying the article showed Leila at her drawing board.

Leila told the reporter about the difficulties involved in achieving her goals: "Many years of preparation are required to become an architect," she said, "while a young woman may learn ste-nography in a much shorter time. Then, after studying architecture, the beginner's pay is poor. It's harder than finding an office job, and

Leila Ross Wilburn during her college years.

such jobs pay much better to begin with. Unless a girl is going to continue at the work, I advise her not to study architecture."

Leila had started her practice in 1909 at age twenty-four. She spent many difficult years developing a clientele. She said, "This experience is compensated for today, however, by the pleasure which comes from building homes." She must have felt completely happy in her vocational choice, because she concluded, "There is nothing I like better, and I don't believe I'd be satisfied with any other job in the world."

Leila Ross Wilburn started life in Macon, Georgia, on November 18, 1885, the first of five children born to Joseph Gustavus Wilburn, an accountant, and Leila Ada Ross, a homemaker and artist. Leila Ross, well educated for her day, had graduated from Wesleyan Female College in 1887 and had later studied at the Pennsylvania Academy of Fine Arts in Philadelphia. At the academy, she had been exposed to some of the nation's most exciting teachers and painters. Her husband's disapproval prevented her from teaching art in Atlanta, but she encouraged her daughter to become an independent woman and study architecture at a time when the profession was just beginning to open up for females.

In 1895 an economic depression sent the Wilburn family to Atlanta, where Joseph sought work. Leila exhibited typical traits of a firstborn child. She was strong-willed, ambitious, determined, focused, and a self-starter. She knew early on what she wanted to do and took purposeful steps to achieve her aim. She attended Agnes Scott Institute (now Agnes Scott College) in Decatur, an Atlanta suburb, from 1903 to 1906. Leila studied the Bible, English, biology, French, history, algebra, and geometry. At the same time, she began what would be her lifelong hobby of observing, photographing, and sketching houses.

Following her graduation from college in 1906, she apprenticed for two years as a draftsperson with Benjamin R. Padgett's architectural and building firm in Atlanta. There she received most of her architecture training.

Leila branched out on her own rather quickly, opening her own business in downtown Atlanta in 1909. "The necessity of economic survival is not known, but it was probably a factor along with the determination to practice architecture," wrote Susan Hunter in her article, "Lady of the House: Leila Ross Wilburn, Architect." In the beginning, Leila designed single-family dwellings and apartments in midtown Atlanta. She would design and build more homes for upper-middle-class clients on Peachtree Street and throughout midtown than any other architect.

Leila Ross Wilburn was the South's second woman architect. Henrietta Cuttino Dozier—the first—had been born in 1872, fifteen years before Leila. Henrietta had an office in the Peters Building, where Leila opened her office, but she left Atlanta a year later. The women traveled different paths to reach their goals: Leila developed her abilities through apprenticeship, whereas Henrietta studied in formal schools of architecture. Both remained single, and both had private practices.

Hunter noted that the practices of Dozier and Wilburn represented the first phase (1895–1920) of women in the architectural profession in Atlanta. "The second phase (1920–1940)," Hunter wrote, "is characterized by a gap filled solely by Wilburn's continued residential practice." The third cycle (1940–1960) brought in a larger group of women, who entered the field at the time the United States entered World War II.

In 1920 Georgia law required architects to register; Leila, the twenty-ninth architect to register with the state that year, was one of only two women who did so. One hundred and sixteen males eventually registered. An architect could work within a private firm without registration, but private practice in the state and advancement within a firm called for registration. Leila did everything she could to ensure her success.

She could not, however, join the AIA (American Institute of Architecture) when it formed its Atlanta chapter in 1909, because she did not meet any of the requirements necessary for charter membership. She was less than thirty years old; she had not graduated from an accredited school of architecture; and she had neither five years of experience as a draftsman nor three years of experience as an architect. She never did join because she did not want to pay the membership dues, and she thought her practice did well enough without AIA endorsement.

The early 1900s was a good time to be an architect. At the time Leila declared herself an independent practitioner, the South was recovering from the depressions of the late 1800s, and Atlanta was experiencing a burst of growth with new buildings springing up everywhere. Members of the upper-middle class were moving to the suburbs, a move enabled by the development of streetcar lines and automobiles. This new market demanded quality homes. The banking and insurance industries were growing and required new buildings. The people working in those fields needed homes, both within the city and in the suburbs.

"Atlanta was undergoing a strong suburban residential building spree," wrote David Ramsay in *The Architecture of Leila Ross Wilburn.* "At this time local writers, real estate developers, and newspapers went to great lengths to sell Atlantans on the idea of a suburban lifestyle and promoted the popular 'back to nature' urge."

"The years immediately preceding World War I were prosperous for Atlantans purchasing their first residential lot," continued Ramsay. "The price of building supplies was low, and a reliable labor force was ready to build. It was under these conditions that Wilburn began her practice and published her first plan book. In sharp contrast, the years between 1915 and 1921 were characterized by a severe building slump. Because of the war effort, building costs for cement and steel soared, while the labor force shrank."

Between 1910 and 1930, the downtown area's increased commercialization continued to push families to the suburbs. Atlanta's growing population led to a severe housing shortage, and relaxed credit requirements made buying a lot and building a home easier than they had previously been.

Leila filled the needs of those wishing to build more than adequately, designing for both private clients and for developers and builders. From 1909 to 1920, she designed eighty homes for single families, twenty-four duplex houses, and twenty apartment buildings with six to twenty-two units each. "Her duplexes, apartment buildings, and single houses were not among the prestigious buildings of the *Southern Architect,* a regional magazine founded in 1889 and edited by Thomas Morgan," wrote Hunter, "but they were the vernacular stuff of Atlanta's real growth in the early twentieth century." She gave her buildings a characteristically Southern essence by using elements such as shed roofs supported by heavy brackets, symmetrical fenestration, porches, and pavilions.

Prior to this period, wealthy people had built ostentatious Victorian homes. By contrast a growing middle class responded positively to Leila's functional, efficient designs that used every inch in the house for a purpose. In her own words, she included, "useful built-in furniture and artistic effects as bookcases, window seats, buffets, plate rails, concealed beds, ironing boards."

In addition to getting ideas from her travels and popular magazines, Leila also studied the works of other architects. She admired Gustav Stickley, for instance, who popularized the Craftsman style, which promoted a comfortable dwelling with an earthy, handmade look. Stickley, editor of the nationally distributed magazine *The Craftsman,* had been influenced by the English Arts and Crafts movement before World War I. Leila added her own touch: "Being a woman, I feel that I know the little things that should go in it to make living in the house a pleasure to the entire family," she said.

"The matching of woman architect and domestic architecture was a natural association, one which Wilburn, in turn, stressed in her marketing rhetoric," wrote Hunter.

In 1914 Leila added a mail-order arm of her business by developing her first planbook. Planbooks were being used in other places around the country, but Leila was the first to use them in Atlanta. She published *Southern Homes and Bungalows,* which contained plans for eighty buildings—and photographs of those buildings—she had designed since 1909. She distributed it to contractors, builders, and developers who would order plans to build themselves or would show the plans to prospective home buyers. The book included plans for Southerners living in the climatic conditions of the Southeast for "moderate-cost residences where the influence of the English half-timber cottage, the Swiss Chalet and the Mission Bungalow is felt." The book served a dual purpose: to disseminate her ideas to the public and to lay a base for her career.

Leila had a good business mind and natural marketing skills. "Wilburn was an unconventional woman, designing and marketing her own product," wrote Hunter. Other established Atlanta architects—all male—had well-known, wealthy clients, so they did not have to rely on their portfolios to attract customers. But Leila was a newcomer and a woman, and for a long time people did not know her or her work; at first, she had few clients. This prompted her to be creative in securing clients and earning her living. When she published her first planbook, she secured ads from businesses related to architecture: construction material firms; contractors and builders; loan companies; and household appliance outlets. Then when the *Atlanta City Directory* came out for that year, she advertised her *Southern Homes and Bungalows,* calling herself a "scientific designer of artistic bungalows." Thus she brought in funds from her earlier house plans to help support her future work.

To keep her name before the public, she advertised widely, including in the *Atlanta Constitution,* the city directory, the *Industrial Index,* and the *Southern Builder.* "The *Atlanta Constitution* frequently published her designs in the Sunday Homes section as appropriate examples of the types of homes suited for Atlanta," Ramsay wrote. Leila even allowed building material advertisers to use her designs as illustrations.

Ramsay points out that Leila's work was not revolutionary and that, because her clients knew current architectural trends in popular literature, she did not exist within a vacuum. "In summary, planbooks gave homeowners the benefit of special architectural services without actually employing an architect," he wrote. They enabled contractors to construct quality suburban developments of impressive variety for the rising middle class. Leila's planbooks were also used by private individuals planning to buy land and build their homes without using an architect.

"She eliminated the . . . relationships between the client, architect, and builder," wrote Ramsay. "The result was a standardized shell offered by Wilburn with freedom left either to the client or builder for ornamental detailing. This freedom, in turn, produced a greater variety amongst her designs."

The planbooks further allowed people to build economical homes that had individual character. The books showed a variety of styles, combining Romantic Revivalism with modern touches drawn together by strong Craftsman principles, producing picturesque neighborhoods. "Leila Wilburn, as a planbook designer," wrote Ramsay, "strove to create an 'Atlantan' character which was generated from nearly 20th Century ideal home philosophies."

Leila even offered practical tips in her planbooks:

"Trees usually enhance the value of the lot . . ."

"East front lots are usually preferred to those facing west."

"Pie-shaped lots are rarely wide enough at the building site."

"A square house is the most economical."

Leila spoke directly to her customers in her planbooks with statements such as "My kitchens are arranged to save extra steps," and "A good home is a debt every man owes his wife." Leila had a twofold purpose in giving her hints. Homeowners or builders received the basic information they needed before buying a piece of property and building a home. Even more important, Leila showed her credibility and insight as an architect who had the consumer's best interest at heart.

"Wilburn's concentration on the needs of the housewife, economics, and character of the home was concurrent with contemporary philosophy at the turn of the century, which focused on the design of domestic space," wrote Ramsay. During the 1880s magazines such as *House Beautiful, Ladies Home Journal, Cosmopolitan,* and *The Craftsman* wrote about simplifying homes. Ramsay continued, "Most Americans wanted private homes that offered health, efficiency, and security . . . that gave a sense of being modern, up to date, social and progressive. It was a challenge to create an elegant, aesthetic but less expensive house with the aim of being a balance between luxury and austerity."

Leila even incorporated some of the phrases used by popular magazines, such as ". . . housewife will appreciate rear stair which connects service portion of house with the front stairs"; "My plans are practical, therefore they save you money"; "Many built-in cupboards are shown"; and "The house is simple in design but not at all severe."

She always emphasized that her designs catered to the Southeast and its climate. Her homes included many windows, sleeping porches, and verandas. As Leila said, "Sunlight is cheaper than doctor's bills."

In 1918 Leila worked for the War Department as a civilian at Fort McPherson in Atlanta. During World War II she worked as an engineering draftsman in Tampa, Florida, and in Washington,

D.C. Hunter wrote, "She is the earliest known woman architect in Georgia to have participated in a war effort and thus she set a precedent for later women who worked for the United States government in the 1940s."

Throughout her career Leila remained dedicated to designing private homes. From 1920 to the 1960s, she designed new styles, slowly changing from Craftsman and Mission bungalows to small Tudor and Jacobean houses and sturdy Colonial and Georgian style houses. The period following World War II found her designing the popular low-slung ranch style homes as well as split-levels. She began to give more attention to low-income single housing units under 1,000 total square feet. In the 1930s Leila started to design homes influenced by the English and French Revival styles.

Leila's homes could be found all over Atlanta, in adjacent Decatur, around Georgia, and throughout the Southeast. Small Southern towns attracted her, and she published designs that would enable a small-town resident to "have a home in as good taste as his city brother."

Her published planbooks include *Southern Homes and Bungalows, Brick and Colonial Homes, Homes in Good Taste, Ideal Homes of Today, Ranch and Colonial Homes, 60 Good Homes, New Homes of Quality,* and *Small Low Cost Homes.*

Leila Wilburn died in 1967 at the age of eighty-two. She had practiced architecture for a total of fifty-eight years, accomplishing a remarkable amount of work. She achieved the distinction of being one of the South's pioneer woman architects, working in a place where all of the other members of her profession were male. Her distinct influence on residential architecture can still be seen in the city of Atlanta.

GERTRUDE "MA" RAINEY
1886–1939

Mother of the Blues

$\mathcal{A}$ccording to the *Dictionary of American Negro Biography*, "In a black theater in 1925, the curtains opened to reveal a huge hand-cranked Victrola. From inside, a gravelly voice sings. Then the doors open, and Ma Rainey steps out. Her gold teeth filling her large mouth sparkle in the blue spotlight. The stage lights give her dark complexion—spread heavily with greasepaint, powder, and rouge to lighten her skin—a golden color."

Although most of the black blues singers were pretty women, Gertrude "Ma" Rainey was a stocky, squat, homely woman. "Black performers said she had 'the ugliest face in show business,'" wrote Sandra Lieb in *Mother of the Blues*. "Thick straightened hair sticking out in all directions, gold caps on her huge teeth, a fan of ostrich plumes in her hand, and a long triple necklace of shiny gold coins reflecting the blue spotlight that danced on her sequined black dress, Ma was a sight to behold."

She dressed in a bright, flashy style, wearing elaborately styled gowns of maroon, blue, or gold beaded satin, sometimes with sequins. She wore glittery jewelry, often donning a famous necklace

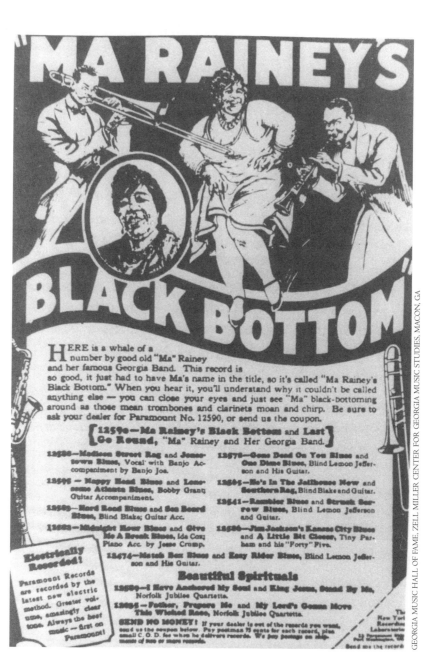

78 rpm sound recording sleeve for "Ma Rainey's Black Bottom."

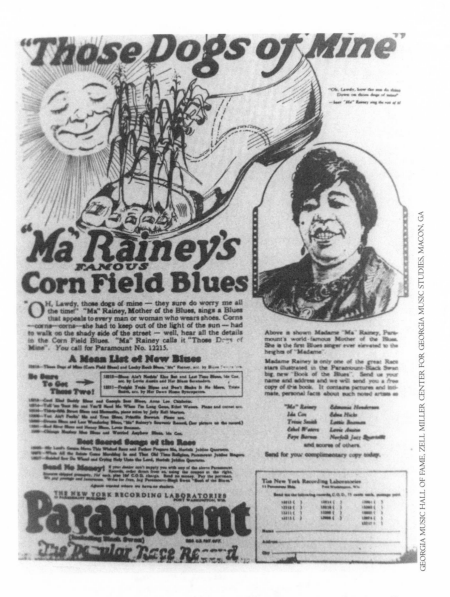

78 rpm sound recording sleeve for "Those Dogs of Mine."

and earrings made of gold pieces, or diamond-studded tiaras, rings, and bracelets.

"[She] was always known as 'Ma' outside her hearing, but in person she preferred to be addressed as 'Madame' Rainey, and in spite of her short stature, her regal bearing and her esteem in which she was held, ensured the respect she wanted," wrote Lieb.

She was also called "Mother of the Blues," "Paramount Wild-cat," and, when she began to carry gold dollars on a chain, the "Gold Necklace Women of the Blues." All titles were appropriate for the unusual and talented singer.

It was at first glance only that people found Ma Rainey unattractive and wild; when she began to sing, they would hear only her beautiful, powerful voice. According to Lieb, trombone player Clyde Bernhardt said, "Yes, she was ugly. But I'll tell you one thing about it; she had such a lovely disposition, you know, and personality, you forget all about it. She commence [sic] to lookin' [sic] good to you."

Thomas A. Dorsey, her pianist on a tour, recalled the excitement of Ma's performance finale. She would step out of the Victrola and "into the spotlight with her glittering gown that weighed twenty pounds and wearing a necklace of five, ten and twenty dollar gold-pieces. The house went wild . . . as if the show had started all over again. . . . They called her the lady with the golden throat. . . . We took seven [curtain] calls."

Ma Rainey was able to connect with the people who came to watch her perform. "Her audiences reacted to her with affection because she maintained a bond with them through her understanding of the blues as she sang," wrote Sharon Harley and Rosalyn Terborg-Penn in *The Afro-American Woman: Struggles and Images.* Lieb commented, "By all accounts, she electrified her audience."

Gertrude Nix Pridgett was born in Columbus, Georgia, on April 26, 1886, the second of five children of Ella and Thomas

Pridgett. She would become the first major woman blues singer in America, and she has been generally credited with the rise in popularity of blues music at the beginning of the twentieth century.

Gertrude may have inherited some of her stage talent from a grandmother who performed onstage after being freed from slavery. Her parents also performed, and Gertrude made her first stage appearance in Columbus at age fourteen with a revue called the Bunch of Blackberries. Gertrude continued to act in tent shows, and even during her most successful days, she preferred to appear under canvas tents rather than in more expensive settings. She liked to be accompanied by a rough jazz band, or even a "jug band"—a band that used homemade instruments such as jugs and washboards.

Gertrude joined Rabbit Foot Minstrels and took her act on the road. A minstrel show was a group of black performers who wore exaggerated black makeup, with broadly painted red lips and white eyes, singing, dancing, and telling jokes in "Negro dialect." Whites had started producing minstrel shows during the 1840s, blacking their faces and "portraying" black life. Around 1855 blacks began to develop their own minstrels and took over the genre.

The Rabbit Foot troupe had its own railroad car, which was attached to a regular train, because "Jim Crow" laws allowed only part of one car to be devoted to black passengers. They carried their own tent, which they set up for one-night performances all over the South, usually following the cotton harvest, when workers had cash. Without microphones, the vocalists developed the ability to project their voices. Gertrude had one of the loudest and best voices—one people did not forget. She did solo acts, calling herself "Madame Gertrude Rainey."

When Gertrude was eighteen, William "Pa" Rainey, an older performer who danced, sang, and did comedy routines came to Gertrude's hometown of Columbus. "Pa" wooed and wed the younger girl on February 1, 1904. The couple developed a song-and-dance team, later calling themselves "Rainey and Rainey, Assassinators of the Blues."

The Raineys adopted a son, Danny, who joined them as a dancer. The couple later separated, and Pa died. "Ma"—who preferred younger men—then remarried a younger man who was not a performer.

While touring in Missouri in 1902 with the Rabbit Foot Minstrels, Gertrude heard the blues for the first time. A local girl sang a plaintive song about the man who had deserted her; the song gripped Gertrude, who learned it and used it in her act. Audiences loved it so much that she began to specialize in singing that type of song. She even claimed that she gave the name "blues" to that type of song, but others said that blues had been around even before Gertrude's birth. An old New Orleans fiddler reportedly said, "The blues? Ain't no first blues! The blues always been." Bunk Johnson, a pioneer bluesman, told an interviewer that he had been playing the blues since his childhood in the 1880s.

Regardless of how blues began, it emerged as a popular type of music in the first three decades of the twentieth century. Southerners, especially blacks from urban areas, embraced the new sound. The blues resembled the mournful songs sung by slaves and black spiritualists. "It combined the black rural traditions of spirituals and work songs with some of the new rhythms being developed by musicians in honky-tonks, bars and brothels," wrote Lieb.

Blues lyrics lamented the misery of having no job and no money or of losing a beloved person—sorrows audiences could relate to. "She [Ma] sang of wandering lives, broken family ties, disappointing love affairs, as well as . . . humor, strength, and resilience in a new environment," wrote Lieb.

Lieb contends that the body of Ma's recorded songs constitutes a message to women, explaining how to deal with reverses in love and how to interpret other areas of life. "In striking contrast to the popular concept of the blues as a music of sorrow and despair, the songs of Ma Rainey reveal an astounding range of emotional reactions to misfortune, from misery to rage and from humor to cynicism," she wrote. "Many songs show women aggressively confronting or attempting to change the circumstances of their lives."

Although Gertrude Rainey probably did not create the name "blues," she helped spread its fame and was the first singer to use blues in minstrel acts. "She appears to be the single or at least the earliest link between the male country blues artists who roamed the streets and back roads of the South and their female counterparts, the so-called 'classic blues' singers," wrote Chris Albertson in *Bessie.*

Gertrude performed in T.O.B.A. (Theatre Owners' Booking Agency) theatres throughout the South. An inside joke said that the initials stood for Tough on Black Artists because the agency's artists often performed in substandard conditions and for very poor pay.

Though outwardly stern, Gertrude was actually a warm and generous person. She behaved maternally toward the younger singers with whom she came into contact. Her loving nature toward children extended beyond her professional life. Over the years she acted as a foster mother to seven children.

Ma Rainey made no secret of the fact that she was bisexual. Her song "Prove It On Me," recorded in 1928, told of her going out with women and included the line, " 'cause I don't like no men." In 1925 police arrested Ma for hosting an "indecent party" after neighbors complained about loud noises. They found a "room full of naked women" in "intimate" situations. When the police arrived, the women grabbed the nearest dresses and raced for the back door. The police caught Ma, the last to leave, when she tripped on the stairs. Ma spent only one night in jail. Friends bailed her out the next morning.

As Ma's star was rising, another young African-American singer appeared on the scene. She was Bessie Smith, and legend says that Ma kidnapped Bessie in Chattanooga, Tennessee, and taught her to sing the blues. The story isn't true, but the two sang together and were close friends. Some even thought they were lovers since both were admittedly bisexual.

Critics thought that Bessie had the superior voice, but Ma gave the greater performance. Poet Sterling Brown recalled: "Ma Rainey was a tremendous figure. She wouldn't have to sing any words; she would moan, and the audience would moan with her. She had them in the palm of her hand. I heard Bessie Smith also, but Ma Rainey was the greatest mistress of an audience. Bessie was the greater blues signer, but Ma really knew these people; she was a person of the folk; she was very simple and direct."

Ma Rainey often performed for segregated audiences. White people (who brought in more revenue) enjoyed her as much as blacks, but she always preferred performing for her own people.

Around 1921 Ma took a brief retirement in Mexico. But further fame and fortune awaited her. Composer-pianist and shrewd businessman Perry Bradford, a Southerner who had spent his early years traveling with minstrel shows and knew the blues tradition, believed strongly that recordings of black music by black performers could sell to Northerners. He persuaded record companies to give it a try.

In 1923, when Ma was age thirty-nine, Paramount Records offered her a contract to record in Chicago, dubbing her "The Mother of the Blues." She recorded more songs for Paramount than any other female star, and along with a male singer, was the company's most popular artist. "In a few short years, she led the transformation of Paramount Records from a subsidiary of a furniture company into a major record label," wrote Tom Sullivan in his essay on Ma.

She received a flat fee per recording session with no royalties, like most other black musicians. Unlike most blues women of her day, she wrote more than a third of the songs she recorded. Some her classics include "C. C. Rider," "Blame It On the Blues," "Bo Weevil Blues," and "Ma Rainey's Black Bottom."

Paramount organized a northern tour for Ma with T.O.B.A. to cash in on her popularity. She toured and recorded from 1924 to 1928, singing with a number of accompanists, including Louis Armstrong.

"Ma Rainey's recordings in 1923 were both a solid artistic achievement and a significant new voice of the rural South," Lieb wrote. "Ma Rainey's [style] . . . brought a rougher, more down-home feeling, with country blues, folk-influenced blues, songs from the minstrel shows, and popular tunes sung in a blues style."

Although Ma earned less money than she would have had she been white, she did well financially. She dressed in gold and diamonds and built a house in Georgia and bought a touring bus. She achieved international fame with the release of her records and was considered to be one of the greatest blues singers by her critics and contemporaries.

Ma recorded twenty titles for Paramount in 1928—the year her fame peaked. Even though her Paramount tour was successful, the company ended her recording contract in 1928, explaining that her down-home, vaudeville material had gone out of style. Ma continued to tour through 1929.

The record company was right. Vaudeville began declining in popularity around 1927. The T.O.B.A. theater performances and classic blues went out of style. Radios and records competed with live music.

In addition, sound had been introduced to motion pictures. In the early days of film, vaudeville acts had played on the same bill with silent films. When talking pictures arrived in 1927, they occupied a theater exclusively, and live entertainment of all kinds had to perform elsewhere.

Work for black blues signers declined. The Depression brought the death knell. The T.O.B.A. theaters closed in June 1930. Ma went back to the minstrel circuit, wearing an imitation pearl necklace rather than the former gold coins. She now traveled in a house trailer rather than the bus, cooking on a small gasoline campstove and canning her own vegetables. It is not certain what happened to her second husband, but a carnival concessionaire traveled with her.

When Paramount declared bankruptcy in the 1930s, Ma's records went out of circulation. In the 1940s and 1950s some of her songs appeared on 78s and long-play albums.

In 1935 Ma retired and returned to Columbus, Georgia. She lived in the house she had built for her family. She had a good business mind and had managed her money well. She operated two theaters she had bought in Rome, in northwest Georgia. Finding comfort from religion, she joined the congregation of the Friendship Baptist Church.

Ma Rainey died from heart disease on December 22, 1939, at the age of fifty-three.

For some reason, the black press ignored her death. Her death certificate—which lists her occupation as housekeeping—likewise did not acknowledge her fame. Time has helped us realize her contribution to American music and culture.

Ma Rainey was inducted into the Blues Foundation's Hall of Fame in 1983 and the Rock and Roll Hall of Fame in 1990 as an "early influence" on the genre. In 1994 a U.S. postage stamp honored Ma Rainey, "Mother of the Blues."

Even with all her fame, Ma always remained loyal to her Southern roots and black audiences.

"Her death came just as collectors and critics were beginning to respond to her individual talent," wrote N. Lee Orr in the *Dictionary of Georgia Biography*.

> She had almost single-handedly forged not only a new type of music but also a new style of performing. She appears to be the earliest link between the less polished music of the country blues of the South and the smoother, more sophisticated blues sound of the more urban 20s and 30s. In fact, the blues claim no real predecessors to her. . . . She probably died unaware that her unique musical expression opened a new field of American music.

LILLIAN SMITH

1897–1966

Conscience of the South

*L*illian Smith wrote, "I was born on the rim of that mysterious terrain which spills over from Georgia's Okefenokee Swamp into Florida. As a child, I walked on earth that trembled." (The Muskogean Indians called the swamp "water shaking.") As an adult, Lillian did some earth shaking of her own through her writing.

Lillian Smith was born on December 12, 1897, in the northern Florida town of Jasper, the seventh of nine children. She grew up in a warm, loving, religious home. Her father, Calvin Warren Smith, a successful businessman and civic leader, provided well for his family. An energetic, intelligent man, he was a devout Methodist. Lillian's mother, Annie Simpson, who had come from a family of wealthy rice planters, had a quieter personality. The family's educational level and wealth gave Lillian a broad outlook on life.

Lillian felt conflict between her parents' religious beliefs and the fact that they practiced racial segregation. She also developed conflicting ideas about her body: though in church they called the human body a "Thing of Shame," she was taught that a white body was superior to one with dark skin. The final conclusion she drew

Lillian Smith

was that not only black people but also any dark idea must be pushed away and repressed.

One particular experience made a deep impression on Lillian. The Smiths brought into their home a white-skinned girl who had been living with a black family. Lillian and the girl became good friends. When the Smiths learned that the child was actually an African American with fair skin, they sent her to a Negro orphanage. Lillian's questions did not bring satisfactory answers. She was told, "A colored child cannot live in our home," or "You're too young to understand;" yet "Aunt Chloe," the family's black nurse, had helped raise Lillian.

While still quite young, Lillian had the ability to empathize with the pain of others, and she seemed to feel that she must observe others and understand them. She felt drawn to both writing and music, showing great talent as a pianist. She practiced the piano six hours a day for about ten years, starting at age eleven.

Lillian wrote in a newspaper column in 1948: "There were good things in that childhood; good sweet things mixed up with the bitter poison of White Supremacy and the awful poverty of so much of our region. And those of us born there, unless hurt too much, still love the sweet and the good, though we fear more and more the poison."

In 1915, the year Lillian graduated from high school, Calvin Smith's businesses failed, so the family moved to north Georgia. Her father opened a small hotel on the site of their summer home on Old Screamer Mountain, and everyone pitched in to operate the inn.

The nearest village, Clayton, provided a sharp contrast to Jasper. Lillian saw poor and poorly educated mountain people walking its muddy streets. The conservative locals were shocked by Lillian's short hair and that she wore short skirts in public.

Lillian seemed to lack a sense of direction during the next few years. She secured a teacher's certificate and taught the next year in a nearby town. Then she entered Piedmont College in another nearby town the year after that. Those two years taught her a lot about mountain people and their plight. She left college to help her parents run a hotel in Daytona Beach, Florida, during the winter of 1916–17.

During this time, Lillian had the only serious romance of her life. The man, a New York violinist twice her age, encouraged her to further her own musical career. His support sent her to study piano at the Peabody Conservatory in Baltimore. While there she nearly starved, but she refused to tell her parents about her economic needs.

By the summer of 1918, her romance had ended. The United States had entered World War I, and Lillian returned to Georgia and joined the Student Nursing Corps. The end of the war ended her connection with the Corps. The next fall she reentered Peabody and stayed there for three years. Even though her instructor considered her to have extraordinary musical talent, Lillian lost confidence in her ability as she compared herself to other students.

In 1922 Lillian went to teach music at a missionary school for wealthy girls in Huchow, China. Her three years there provided her with the most profound experiences of her life, awakening her political awareness. She observed colonialism, racism, and an acceptance of white supremacy, all of which reminded her of the way she saw whites treating blacks in the southern United States. She wrote, "For the first time in my life I was ashamed of my white skin." She also became an agnostic during this time.

Concern for her parents' health and financial well-being brought her back home in 1925. She saw with new eyes the problems of poor blacks and poor white mountain people. It fell to her to direct the summer camp for girls her father had opened at the hotel near Clayton. This type of work did not match her talents or interests, and she felt that some counselors encouraged girls to form homosexual attachments to them. Taking care of the practical problems relating to operating a camp took most of Lillian's time. She felt the work brought out what she called her "Martha" side (her practical aspects), while doing nothing to enrich her "Mary" side (her idealistic aspects) as China had.

She wrote: "Those were miserable, even nightmarish years for me. . . . What did I care [about a camp]? . . . then Mary began nudging me: 'you can make this camp experience as creative as a poem, a piece of music, a novel.' . . . And the nightmare began to turn into something . . . even wonderful at times."

Lillian began by beautifying the unfinished camp property. Over the next ten years, she changed the camp's emphasis from competitiveness in sports to creativity, instituting reading, creative writing, drama, modern dance, painting, sculpture, and etching classes.

"To put it simply, Miss Lil was fascinating," wrote Kathryn Palumbo in her article "Summers of Yesteryear at Laurel Falls Camp." "Her warm brown eyes and honey-colored hair framed a face always ready to give a wink and a smile."

Lillian studied Freudian psychology and used Freud's concepts in her work with the girls. She wrote:

We talked about the body and its functions and . . . went into sex, especially the matter of babies, etc; . . . we talked about our hopes and dreams, how hard a relationship can be between a girl and mother, sometimes girl and father, often a girl and her sisters and brothers. . . . We spoke of hate as . . . natural. . . . We talked about envy, jealousy . . . etc.; we talked about ideals and the difference in an ideal and a guilt feeling. . . . We went out into the world beyond our mountain and talked about war and peace, racial problems, poverty, class snobbery, conformity, acceptance of differences.

Lillian wanted to help the girls grow emotionally and intellectually as well as physically, as had been her father's emphasis. In order to promote race relations, she wanted to invite black campers, but the girls' parents would not allow it. Lillian did invite black mothers and daughters for a lunch at the camp, which was a bold practice at that time.

She also invited Paula Snelling, a high school mathematics teacher, to join her at the camp. Under their leadership, Laurel Falls Camp became known as one of the best for girls in the South. She and Paula remained friends for life.

In the fall of 1925, Lillian again turned her back on her own needs and went to Fort Pierce, Florida, to take care of her niece following the death of her brother's wife. She stayed there for two winters.

Next, she spent the winter semesters of 1927 and 1928 at Columbia University Teachers College in New York. She studied history, education, and psychology, as well as public school music. The music course led her to teach in a Harlem school where, for the first time, she worked with black students. Although she never graduated from college, she educated herself in psychology, anthropology, history, sociology, philosophy, religion, and literature.

In the summer of 1928 she bought Laurel Falls Camp from her father. In 1930 Calvin Smith died of cancer, and Lillian took over the care of her mother. She began to write materials for the camp, which led to a desire to write more. But what else could she write about? After several attempts in other directions, she decided to write disguised accounts of her own life. She first wrote a novel based on her experiences in China, describing it as "soft, warm, passionate, vivid, naked, honest, lyrical." The book "scared the publishers to death," she said. Two publishers rejected it.

Paula invited Lillian to spend the winters of 1930 to 1935 with her in Macon, Georgia, where Paula taught high school. Lillian wrote more regularly while there. Studying Freud helped her release some of her guilt feelings with regard to her family.

In 1935 Lillian again turned aside her own needs when her mother had a heart attack. She moved from Macon back to Old Screamer Mountain and took care of her mother for the next three years. Lillian felt resentful, yet she gave in to her "Martha" side and did what she considered to be the "right" thing.

During these years she drafted a novel on China, a novel about a Southern family, and a novella. A 1944 fire destroyed those manuscripts along with other precious items. She also worked during that time on the manuscript that would become her first published book.

Lillian called 1935 "a mean bad year." In addition to taking care of her mother on Old Screamer, she brought Paula to the house to recover from a nearly fatal fall from a horse. As these two creative women became increasingly bored, Lillian conceived the idea of starting a magazine. Lillian became a published writer for the first time when they produced the magazine first called *Pseudopodia*, named for the "extra" foot of the amoeba. The women defined it as "a temporary and tender projection of the nucleus of the inner-self, upon the success of whose gropings the nucleus is entirely dependent for its progress and sustenance."

The magazine, which they finally named *South Today*, began as a quarterly and then changed to a semiannual production. The first issue had just twenty-seven subscribers, but circulation grew to nearly ten thousand. The magazine served as an outlet for lesser known writers and focused on life in the South. It was the only Southern journal of its type that published and reviewed the work of black writers. The two women never paid themselves anything for their work. Imprisoned in the Georgia mountains, they brought the outside world to them. They paid their writers by inviting them for a week's vacation at the camp. These invitations resulted in integrated house parties, which were illegal at the time because of Georgia's segregation laws. Luckily, the local sheriff admired the two women and ignored their activities.

Lillian wrote a regular column for the magazine and contributed some of her fiction. Believing in literature's ability to help solve race problems, she urged writers to use their skills in this direction. Wanting to get to know the South better, Lillian traveled through the southern states, interviewing people, and reading everything she could on the subject.

After Lillian's mother died in 1938, Lillian and Paula spent three months in Brazil, where they observed similar social conditions to those present in the South.

The war climate in Europe occupied Lillian's efforts as the 1930s came to a close. She opposed the United States entering the war, insisting that Americans needed to work on the threats to democracy and freedom at home, especially with respect to blacks, before spreading democracy abroad.

Next, the two women received fellowships from the Rosenwald Fund that allowed them to travel around the South for two years, visiting people in every economic level, from truck drivers to union leaders. Lillian said, "I broke every barrier I could . . . to see 'things as they are.'" For the first time, she talked with educated blacks. Between 1942 and 1944, the women visited some Negro colleges and universities as members of the Rosenwald Scholarship Committee.

Increasingly Lillian changed her focus from literary efforts to battling segregation and racial discrimination. She began in quiet ways, such as inviting blacks to her camp, working in

Harlem, visiting black schools in the South, and featuring black authors in the magazine.

Lillian and Paula held their first major biracial gathering in the fall of 1936. In the fall of 1942, they invited twenty-four women of both races for a four-day "camp." Over the years, a wide range of guests came to the camp: people of opposite political positions, of different races and nationalities, of different economic and education levels.

Lillian and Paula wrote an editorial in a 1942 issue of *South Today* declaring that blacks should receive treatment equal to whites. Though she spoke of the hurts segregation brought to blacks, she believed that it hurt whites even more, saying that it stunted the emotional growth of whites. She wrote, "It would be difficult to decide which character is maimed the more, the white or the Negro, after living a life in the southern framework of segregation." She urged individuals to do small acts on their own as well as take part in organized efforts.

In February 1944 Lillian's first novel, *Strange Fruit,* was published. The title came from a phrase she had used in a 1941 article in her magazine describing the "strange fruit" produced by Southern old-time religion.

The book dealt with the romance between a white man and a black woman in the fictional town of Maxwell, Georgia, which Lillian based on Jasper, Florida. It caused quite a stir, even though Lillian maintained that she had not purposely written "a race book." Her broader concern was about how people dehumanize themselves and each other. She saw segregation as a wall between people, one which she had fought against since coming back from China in 1925.

The book received primarily negative reviews in the South, but readers around the nation bought enough copies to place the book on the bestseller list of the *New York Times Book Review.* Boston banned the book in March, objecting to its obscene language. Two months later, the U.S. postal service banned it from the mail. Eleanor Roosevelt, who liked the book, asked the president to intervene, and the ban, which increased sales, was lifted. Most critics saw the book as an effort to improve race relations rather than as literature, a fact that distressed Lillian. The book eventually sold three million copies, was made into a Broadway play, and was translated into sixteen languages.

The income from the book enabled Lillian to make improvements at the camp and to pay off the mortgages on the camp and her summer home. By that time, Lillian had also achieved national fame through the magazine.

In 1946 the British government hosted Lillian on a visit to India as a member of the Famine Commission. Her second visit there in 1954–55 with Paula inspired her to write a book about Prime Minister Jawaharlal Nehru. A 1955 fire destroyed her notes for the book along with other valuable papers. Letters she had received from Eleanor Roosevelt—the person she admired more than anyone else—also burned in the fire.

In 1947 Lillian began working on a nonfiction book on segregation, *Killers of the Dream,* in which she applied Freud's theories to the South. It was her most significant writing, and, like all others, was autobiographical. She was disappointed in its lukewarm reception, concluding that reviewers had misunderstood it.

In the fall of 1949, she and Paula stopped publishing their magazine. To fill her time, Lillian wrote articles, made speeches about racism, and took part in several organizations. Income from *Strange Fruit* allowed her to close the camp. Lillian received two honorary doctorates in 1950.

Lillian rejected society's taboos in all areas. She had dealt with lesbianism in her first two books, and many people thought that Lillian and Paula had a lesbian relationship. A male friend said he saw no indications of that. Lillian had had affairs with men when she was younger. Lillian said that Paula helped nourish her "Mary" side, which helped her become a better writer. Lillian felt she was living an almost total "Martha" existence while running the camp. Paula encouraged her to read and discuss books.

In 1953 Lillian started writing a nonfiction book called *The Journey.* In the prologue, she wrote, "I went on this journey to find an image of the human being that I could feel proud of." Her journey led her to believe in the dignity of man and to return to religious faith, although she did not define this faith precisely, except to say that it included a belief in God. Her own faith was tested that year when she learned she had breast cancer. After an operation, she completed the book, which was published in 1954.

At that time, she went to work trying to persuade whites to move forward in the area of race relations, writing letters and inviting people to Old Screamer for conversations. She wrote *Now is the Time,* a small book intended to inspire people to want to end segregation.

Early in 1955 Lillian went to India for a six-month research trip. Upon her return, she was dismayed to learn that her cancer had returned. Following her successful surgery and x-ray treatment, she spent a month as writer in residence at Vassar College. It was there that she received the distressing news that a fire at Old Screamer had destroyed her bedroom and study.

The fire also destroyed thirteen thousand letters, manuscripts of three novellas, the only two copies of a novel she had written about China, outlines for future writing, all her research materials from India, and her personal effects. Lillian could only wonder if the fire, set by two white boys, related to her work. Some biracial gatherings had taken place there shortly before the fire, and Lillian thought those events had disturbed locals. Her output as a writer possibly would have been much greater if the two fires had not destroyed much of her work.

Lillian retreated to her brother's fishing camp in Florida, stating her intention to go ahead and write the book on India. While recovering from the trauma of the fire, she learned that the publisher of *Now is the Time* was evidently yielding to pressure and withdrawing the book. Thereafter, she curtailed her writing and speaking activities.

Back in Georgia, she started working on a novel, *One Hour.* She and Paula became concerned about their safety in their isolated setting on Old Screamer. In 1958 fires were set on the mountain twice, and strangers would drive up the mountain at night.

In the late 1950s Lillian emphasized two new paths in her views on race relations. First, partly because of what she called her "smothering," and partly responding to Senator Joseph McCarthy's activities, she called for freedom of speech. Second, she felt afraid of what she saw as the "mob" response to progress in race, with people regressing to primitive fears and actions. She began to lose her lifelong optimism that progress in Southern race relations could be obtained. Martin Luther King, Jr.'s rise to leadership renewed her hope. She also saw hope in the idea of recruiting young people to work in the movement toward integration.

Like *Strange Fruit, One Hour* told a love story about a young couple in the South. This book did not deal with race but instead explored the issue of how difference of any kind scares people. A theme of the book is hope, which Lillian included to counteract what she saw as a current wave of nihilism. To her surprise, Southerners received the book well. Even Clayton residents read it!

She started writing a sequel to the book and continued work on a new project, *Julia.* She also agreed to write a book for the World Perspective series. Research for that project prompted her to seek answers to questions she had about philosophy and religion. Through her friendship with the intellectual theologian Paul

Tillich and through reading his books, she began to get in touch with the faith of her childhood.

The 1960s found Lillian getting involved in the civil rights movement. That and the reaction to *One Hour* led her to think that the public had stereotyped her only as a person who helped Negroes, rather than seeing her as a total person, an intelligent woman.

She next wrote *Our Faces, Our Words,* which contained fictionalized monologues based on her interviews of many young people who were active in the civil rights movement. Photographs accompanied the text.

In early 1966 an *Atlanta Constitution* editorial spoke of Lillian as ". . . one of the nation's most distinguished writers, a woman who loves the South and has worked for both Negroes and whites all her life. . . ." Lillian Smith died on September 28, 1966. She was buried amid the dogwood and rhododendron on Old Screamer. The words on her headstone read: "Death can kill a man. That is all it can do to him. It cannot end his life because of memory."

In *Lillian Smith: A Southerner Confronting the South,* Anne C. Loveland summed up her extensive work:

> Of the small group of white southerners who enlisted in the civil rights movement in the 1930's, she is now hailed as one of the first to speak out publicly against racial segregation. . . . Historians now recognize Lillian Smith as a pivotal fixture in southern intellectual life as the region emerged from the renaissance years into the turmoil of the civil rights revolution.

LEILA DAUGHTRY DENMARK
1898–

Centenarian Pediatrician

*T*he pictures of Dr. Denmark's patients, whom she called "the little angels," still hang in the foyer of her office, now closed. Letters, poems, and cards from her many patients' families crowd the waiting room walls. When the office was open, patients waited on old church pews, and Dr. Denmark examined babies on the old wooden examination table that she had used since she first graduated from medical school. She had no receptionist or nurse and took no appointments, taking patients in the order in which they arrived. Dr. Denmark greeted them with, "Who's the next angel?"

Dr. Denmark practiced medicine long enough to treat three generations of patients in the same families. One time, a man, age sixty-four, who had been a patient in the 1930s, came in with his daughters—themselves former patients—who brought their children.

One mother started taking her baby to Dr. Denmark on the recommendation of her gas station attendant! When the woman first took her baby to the doctor's office, she found the sign CLOSED THURSDAYS on the door. Seeing a big white house next door, she took a chance that it was the doctor's home and knocked on the

Leila Daughtry in 1917.

door. Dr. Denmark took the baby over to the office and spent two hours with the mother.

Church friends urged another woman to take her baby to Dr. Denmark, but the mother felt reluctant at first to do so because of the doctor's advanced age. She finally went and sang the doctor's praises afterward.

Children have said that going to Dr. Denmark's office was like going to a favorite grandmother's house. Even her appearance is grandmotherly. She pulls her white hair back and ties it tightly into a bun. Her brown eyes shine as brightly as a younger person's. At five feet tall, she stands erect; although she may look frail, she actually is feisty.

Leila Alice Daughtry was born on February 1, 1898, in Bulloch County, twelve miles west of Portal in south Georgia. She was the third of twelve children in the family of Elerbee and Alice Hendricks Daughtry. The family raised cotton and other crops as well as animals on the four hundred–acre farm that had been in the family for several generations.

Dr. Denmark speaks highly of her parents and the influence they had on her. Both parents had even tempers and behaved in a well-mannered way toward their children. Self-educated Elerbee Daughtry read voraciously.

Dr. Denmark recalled with gratitude the excellent nursing care she received from her mother when she was sick as a child: hot baths, clean sheets, quietness, good food, and cheerful words. Even though she had to take care of twelve children, her mother never was in a hurry or lost her temper.

Apparently Leila took after her mother. When parents would ask Dr. Denmark, "What makes my children so bad?" the doctor, known for her blunt speaking, would answer, "Go look in the mirror. You get apples off apple trees."

Leila's mother let her daughters learn to sew as soon as they were tall enough to operate the foot pedal on the sewing machine. After Leila learned to sew, she thought that clothing design would be her career, so she taught herself to make hats. After learning to cook, she thought she would become a dietitian.

When asked the question, "What led you to become a doctor?" Dr. Denmark answered: "When I was a child on the farm, I always liked to see things live. Something was always going wrong with animals. For example, a big rain would get the little biddies [baby chicks] wet, and if any got sick as a result, I would take care of them." She also learned gardening from her mother, rescuing any flowers that someone else had thrown out and bringing them back to life.

When Leila was young, a Dr. Bowen lived behind her family's property. When Leila's mother called him about a sick family member, he would ask her what she thought was wrong and what they ought to do, and then he would do what she recommended. "Alice did the doctoring," Leila concluded. Dr. Bowen later encouraged Leila to attend medical school. When Leila became a doctor, she encouraged mothers to trust their own instincts about raising their children.

Because Leila couldn't walk fast enough to keep up with her older sisters as they trekked to school, her mother taught her at home until she was eight. Then Leila walked 2½ miles to the local two-room school that went through the sixth grade. One farm separated the Daughtry farm from the Denmark farm, and Eustace Denmark—whom Leila would marry later—and his siblings walked along with the Daughtry children.

When the railroad went through the farming area where Leila grew up, the town of Portal, Georgia, was created. Leila's father served as mayor of the town for thirty-five years. The city fathers opened a school over the bank, and Leila attended classes there until the tenth grade.

Leila then enrolled in a boarding high school in nearby Statesboro. At school, she wore a uniform consisting of a navy skirt, a white middy blouse, and a navy tie. There she "became a great tennis player," she boasted. Because she is left-handed, opponents had trouble returning her serves!

She then went to Bessie Tift College in Forsyth, Georgia, graduating in 1922. She earned the nickname "Doc" from her friends because of her intense interest in anatomy and dissection. In fact, one of her teachers created a lab in which she could dissect frogs.

During the four years she attended college, Leila taught Sunday school in a cotton mill village mission. She noticed the children there had several problems: They lacked motivation to study; the boys were generally troublemakers; and they were thin and had poor appetites. The girls married young, repeating the habits of their mothers, especially those of smoking, chewing tobacco, and/or dipping snuff. Leila decided to study the children in hope that she could find a way to help them.

When Leila was twenty-two, her mother died at age forty-six of uterine cancer. Her father remarried.

After college, Leila gave up the idea of entering medicine because she had school debts to pay. Instead, she took a train to a rural village north of Atlanta to teach elementary school. When she arrived, a man, upon learning why she had come, said, "Miss Daughtry, you're going to teach the meanest boys on earth. They've run off lots of teachers." Leila didn't know what the man was talking about until she entered the classroom and found she was the smallest person in the group! This one hundred–pound woman had male students who were taller, bigger, and much stronger than she was. She won them over, however, and never had any trouble from them the two years she taught there.

In that mill village, she continued to study the effects of tobacco on the residents.

Leila considered going to India as a medical missionary to women, but her engagement to Eustace Denmark in the early 1920s changed those plans. In 1924 Eustace went to Java, Indonesia, for two years as a vice-consul in the U.S. Consular Service. Leila agreed to wait for him and spent that first summer studying physics and chemistry at Mercer University in Macon.

In the fall of 1924, she enrolled at the Medical College of Georgia. "At that time, even nursing was considered 'a disgraceful occupation' for a 'nice' woman," she remembered with a smile. She was the only female in her class. She graduated in 1928, the third woman to graduate from a medical school in Georgia.

Although Eustace Denmark returned from Indonesia in 1926, the couple waited to get married until Leila had graduated. The ceremony was held at noon so neighboring farmers could attend and then return to their fields. The groom was twenty-nine, the bride thirty.

The couple moved to Atlanta, where Eustace worked in the Georgia State Banking Department. In the summer of 1928, Leila started her internship in the segregated black wards at Grady Hospital. She also interned for six months at Children's Hospital in Philadelphia. She then became the first intern at the newly opened Henrietta Egleston Hospital for Children. For the next fifty-seven years she donated her services to the Central Presbyterian Church charity baby clinic.

At the clinic Dr. Denmark continued to study the effects of tobacco on parents and children and developed a firm position against any use of tobacco by anyone.

Leila and her husband lived in an Atlanta apartment after their marriage. After their daughter Mary's birth in 1930, they rented a house. Dr. Denmark set up an office in the breakfast room so she could watch her baby and her caretaker out the window while she worked. When Mary was three, the Denmarks bought their first house. Patients waited in the living room there, and Dr. Denmark used the den as an examining room.

Dr. Denmark always had domestic help in the house—such services could be secured cheaply during the Depression era. Until Mary entered school, Dr. Denmark had live-in help; from then on, she had help twelve hours a day.

In the late 1940s the Denmarks built a home in Sandy Springs, an Atlanta suburb, with an office adjacent to the carport. The doctor saw patients there for thirty-six years. Every evening, Dr. Denmark went directly home to supper with her family.

Later on the family bought property "way out in the country" north of Atlanta and built a house. The property also included a 150-year-old log house covered with wood siding. "The house was a shack," Dr. Denmark recalled. "Bootleggers had lived there and had shot holes in the ceilings and walls." Her grandson Steven helped to renovate it for her to use as an office. "I asked him to make one room into a den for me with a sofa where I could lie down and rest." She added with a grin, "I never used it once." Although the sign on the door read OFFICE HOURS: 8:00 A.M.–3:00 P.M., she often worked there until after eight o'clock at night. "I worked from the time I opened until I finished," she said.

In 1932 Dr. Denmark read a few lines in the *Journal of the American Medical Association* about a doctor speculating on a possible vaccine for whooping cough. A recent outbreak of seventy-five cases in Atlanta had led to some deaths, so Leila decided to do more research.

After hearing about a man near Atlanta who had a severe case of whooping cough, she went to his house and asked for some of his blood. She put the 100 cc's in the icebox, and then injected a child who had whooping cough subcutaneously with it the next morning. The child had a remarkable recovery, and Dr. Denmark knew she was on to something important. She further learned that if a mother had had whooping cough, she could inject the mother's blood into the child to cure the child.

She wrote the Eli Lilly Company about her research and asked them if they would make a vaccine she could test. After vaccinating hundreds of kids with the serum they produced, she asked Eli Lilly to double the strength, which the company did. She gives credit to the company and others who helped.

Although some critics say the vaccine can cause dangerous reactions, Dr. Denmark used it from 1932 until 2001 without ever having a patient suffer a serious reaction. If a child had any reaction, he also had something else wrong with him that produced the reaction, she found. The serum is still used today.

In 1935 Dr. Denmark received the Fisher Award for outstanding research in diagnosis, treatment, and immunization of whooping cough. The pertussis vaccine is given routinely to infants in DTP shots. (The Fisher Award is given annually for the most outstanding medical research in Atlanta.)

Dr. Denmark is passionate—and outspoken—about her beliefs that mothers need to stay at home with their children, even though she knows these views are often unpopular. She believes that no matter what college degrees mothers have, it's absolutely vital to children's health and well-being that mothers invest their time and energies at home, particularly when children are young. "Rearing children is the most important work on earth," the doctor maintains. "It's the hardest job and the biggest one. It should be the most elevated."

In fact, she said, that position was the reason she had to self-publish her book. Publishers rejected it because she was not supporting women working outside the home.

"A woman can do anything," she said. "She could be president of the United States as far as I'm concerned. But if she brings a baby into the world, she should take responsibility for it."

It distresses her that the majority of children spend most of their waking hours in day care.

Dr. Denmark urges mothers to trust themselves and "to use their own minds." "When I was a young doctor, I used to meet with new parents at the hospital after the baby arrived . . . ," she wrote. "I said to the mother . . . 'You will have everybody telling you how to rear your child. . . . Go home and do just what you think is best.'"

Leila's daughter, Mary Hutcherson, reflected, "Mother felt that a doctor's word was not necessarily the last word, that parents had the good sense to raise a child."

"Nurse your baby if possible," Dr. Denmark advocates. "For your own sake as well as your infant's, don't be in a hurry to get back to a full schedule after giving birth. Rest as much as you can for at least two weeks. Staying quietly at home helps both mother and baby," she wrote.

She urges parents to let babies cry. "It won't hurt [a newborn baby] to cry. Actually, it is absolutely necessary that [he] cry. It helps clean out the baby's nose and strengthens the lungs."

"Mother has a good analytical mind, which made her a good diagnostician," Mary said. "Her emphasis in medicine was not to treat symptoms but to try getting to root causes of sickness and then solving the problem. . . . Mother was blunt speaking to parents when it came to the welfare of their children. She would say, 'You know what you're doing is not right,' especially if a parent smoked, for example. Some people didn't return because they didn't like her message."

Dr. Denmark believes, "A child should be taught by word and example the religion the parents believe in."

"Mother had a strong religious background and has always attended church," Mary said. "She is reticent about speaking about her faith, though. I believe that in the business of healing the sick, she practiced her faith."

Dr. Denmark believes that the promises of the suffragettes—whom she supported—have not materialized. "They promised wonderful things, tremendous change if and when they won the vote," she said. "Well, they won the vote, but they have not gotten rid of tobacco and alcohol and bad politics." She said, "We need to give a child safety, love, and a sense of trust." She added, "We women have had the vote since 1922, but we have less of all of the above."

When asked about her work, Dr. Denmark replied: "I've never *worked*. I've *played* all these years. Anything you *have* to do is work, what you *love* to do is play. Therefore I've *played* all my life. I've never been tired," she declared. "My husband used to say that I'd come home tired in the evening, and someone would call about a baby, and I'd be sixteen again!"

Dr. Denmark has always taken good care of her health. In the 1950s she and her husband started playing golf on vacations, and she played until September 2000. In her younger years, she enjoyed hiking and horseback riding. She hiked up LeConte Mountain in North Carolina and even once rode a horse up one of the trails.

Her grandsons were still pushing her to hike at age ninety. She continued walking to the lake on her property and back each day—more than a mile round trip—until her eyesight failed.

When she was young, she loved to eat sugar. "Nobody could make better pound cakes than I could," she remembered with a smile. "I was always eating something sweet." By age thirty-five, she had developed arthritis and had sore joints and pain in her hips. At age fifty, she eliminated sugar from her diet, using only a little honey now and then. Her sore joints disappeared, and at age one hundred, she could touch the floor without bending her knees. "I don't know if there is a correlation between my sugar intake and the arthritis, but I believe there was."

When offered a piece of birthday cake at her one hundredth birthday party, she replied, "Oh, no, thank you. I haven't knowingly eaten sugar for over sixty-five years." She gave up coffee in 1962 after she developed arthralgia, and the symptoms went away. "If only people could just use their brains about eating," she said.

She laughs, "When I die, I'm going to will my heart to a ten-year-old boy!"

Dr. Denmark has always loved to make things. She made every lampshade in her house and nearly every dress she has ever owned.

"I bought six dresses along the way," she said, "but I never wore them." She did wear one bought dress, her blue silk wedding dress that her older sister bought for her. A framed snapshot on the mantel in her home shows her and her husband as newlyweds.

Even though she is a home-loving person, Dr. Denmark has traveled extensively, including trips to Canada, Alaska, the Northwest, and South America. Onboard a ship for a trip at age sixty-one she became determined to learn to swim. Because she had never learned to swim as a child, she had nightmares about kids drowning and not being able to save them. She borrowed her daughter's bathing suit, and even though her sister and Eustace thought she had lost her mind, she got up early so no one would see her and began to teach herself. After ten days, she could swim the pool's length. And she never had another nightmare.

Leila and Eustace Denmark had a very happy marriage. "We never had any trouble at all. I listened carefully to what he said, and then I did what I pleased," she said wryly. "We never argued. Why argue with anyone? 'A man convinced against his will is of the same opinion still.'" She stated firmly, "Eustace was the greatest man who ever lived."

Although history names Dr. Denmark's greatest accomplishment as her help in developing the pertussis vaccine, she said her greatest accomplishment was getting Eustace as a husband. Mercer University honored the couple in 1987 as lifetime members of the President's Club. Mercer also gave Leila an honorary doctor of science degree in 1991.

Eustace died of congestive heart failure in 1990 at age ninety-one after sixty-two years of marriage. "My parents were very compatible and complemented each other in many ways," Mary said. "Mother had no interest in business and since Daddy worked in Federal Reserve Banking, he handled the family money and investments and served as her business manager. Both parents had a good sense of humor." Mary still takes her mother to North Carolina each year for one round of golf.

In May 2001 Dr. Denmark developed two medical problems. "When you drive a car 103 years, the tires get thin," she said with a grin. She had a medical procedure to repair a collapsed vertebra. The doctor injected "cement" to prop up the vertebra, "similar to a dentist filling a tooth."

The doctor tried to talk Dr. Denmark out of having the procedure because of her age, predicting that her bones would be so soft the surgery would simply be impossible.

After the operation he told her, "Your bone was the hardest I've ever dealt with. I could hardly get through it."

Dr. Denmark explained, "Because I've always worked in the garden, I've gotten plenty of Vitamin D. That's where I get my strong bones."

At the same time, however, Dr. Denmark also developed macular degeneration. She closed her practice, fearing that her loss of vision might prevent her from accurately diagnosing a child's condition. At the time she retired she was America's oldest working doctor.

She still lives in her impressive colonial-style home, sleeping in her second-floor bedroom, which means that she climbs eighteen steps daily. She uses a hiking stick as she walks around the house.

Mary spends every Thursday with her mother, bringing videos of old movies to watch. She takes her grocery shopping and cooks batches of food that Dr. Denmark heats the rest of the week, praising her microwave oven. "It if weren't for Mary, I'd have to be in a nursing home," she said. "Not being able to read is the worst part about my failing eyesight." She likes her independence, space, and light, and the amenities she would not have in a nursing home. Her home has many large windows that bring in a great deal of light.

Sitting in a recliner chair with her feet propped up, Dr. Denmark still remains available for telephone consultation for parents with medical questions. She is still speaking her message: "The hardest job on this earth, and the most important, is mothering. It's twenty-four hours a day for twenty-one years. Nowadays we have everything under the sun to keep children healthy—money, medicines, good food—everything but parents."

MARGARET MITCHELL
1900–1949

Author of the World's Favorite Novel

$\mathcal{O}$ne hot September day in 1906, petite Margaret Mitchell refused to return to first grade, saying she hated arithmetic and already knew what they tried to teach her. Her mother, Maybelle, put her obstinate daughter into her horse and buggy and took her on a spirited ride around Jonesboro, her hometown south of Atlanta. She pointed out old, decrepit houses destroyed by the Civil War followed by equally old but well-kept houses. Some people had survived the effects of the war while others had not. The difference, Maybelle thundered, was education. "People—and especially women—might as well consider they are lost without an education. . . . For all you're going to be left with after your world upends will be what you do with your hands and what you have in your head. You will go back to school tomorrow."

Thirty years later, Margaret's novel *Gone with the Wind* was published in hard cover; it became the most famous novel in the English-speaking world. Margaret said: "If the novel has a theme it is that of survival. What makes some people able to come through catastrophes and others, apparently just as able, strong and

Margaret Mitchell poses with her bestselling novel.

brave, go under? . . . I only know that the survivors used to call that quality 'gumption.' So I wrote about the people who had gumption and the people who didn't."

Margaret's family had gumption, especially her maternal grandmother, Annie Stephens, in whose Atlanta home Margaret was born on November 8, 1900. A second theme of the book is love of the land, a love that Margaret's family embraced.

As Margaret grew up, she was collecting information that helped her create the characters and the plot of her novel. Some students of her work say that the book is actually an autobiography of Margaret herself set in an earlier time. The daughter of attorney Eugene Mitchell, Margaret was born into a family that had shaped Atlanta's history for five generations. Her ancestors had lived through the Civil War and Reconstruction. Confederates had used the Stephens's house as a hospital during the Battle of Atlanta. Margaret and her friends staged mock battles and found cannonballs and bullets in the old Confederate breastworks behind her grandmother's house.

Margaret heard family members talking constantly of the war and the years following. She recalled: "On Sunday afternoons when we went calling on the older generation of relatives, those who had been active in the Sixties [1860s], I sat on the bony knees of veterans and the fat slippery laps of great aunts and heard them talk." She also enjoyed listening to others who told stories about the Confederate veterans and the War Between the States.

Margaret adored, yet feared, her strong-willed mother, Maybelle, a devout Catholic who did a tremendous amount of charitable work even though she had fragile health. From about 1900 until her death in 1919, Maybelle devoted her energies to the women's suffrage movement, strapping baby Margaret on her hip while attending some meetings. She founded the more liberal wing of the suffragette movement that became the League of Women Voters.

Several factors influenced the child who would become an outstanding writer. Maybelle encouraged her daughter to read the classics and write her own stories. Margaret became an avid reader, but, strong-willed like her mother, Margaret defied Maybelle's orders to read the classics, choosing to be spanked with a slipper rather than obey. Instead, she read fairy tales and books about the Rover boys. As she grew older, she read Victorian novels, detective stories, and murder mysteries, and developed a passion for pulp fiction. She smuggled books into bed, reading them by flashlight. One of her older brother's earliest memories was seeing her "in a starched dress, her short blonde hair brushed back from her face, sitting on the top step of the porch deep in a book" at their home.

Margaret and her mother continually clashed about Margaret's schooling. She did poorly in French, geometry, and Latin, but did well in history. In English, she loved reading, writing, and literature; but she couldn't muster up the discipline needed for spelling, grammar, and syntax.

She wrote hundreds of stories before she was twelve. Only four still exist. She used dialogue well, a skill unusual in young writers, and showed a mastery of language and an ability to create plots. She created plays from her writings that she presented with neighborhood children. She told stories extremely well, too.

As a young adult, she became fascinated by books on the history of the South. She read rapidly, and by the time she was twenty-one she had read every book on Southern history in the Atlanta Public Library.

During her life, she became one of the greatest letter writers of the century, sometimes corresponding at great length to friends, family, sweethearts, and servicemen she helped during World War

11. After the publication of her book, she wrote hundreds of letters to fans, answering every letter she received.

As Margaret grew up, she showed an independent, vivacious, witty personality. During high school, she gave herself a new name: Peggy. Young men pursued the flirty, charming Peggy, and several soldiers fell in love with her at the beginning of World War I. At age seventeen she became engaged to Lt. Clifford Henry of New York before he left for service overseas.

After Peggy graduated from high school, Mrs. Mitchell enrolled her daughter in Smith College in Northampton, Massachusetts, because the school believed women should have educational opportunities equal to men's. She did poorly in her studies, and friends remembered her as being a clown who broke rules and entertained them with enthralling Civil War tales. Years later, she wondered if she had been on the edge of having a nervous breakdown during that time.

Peggy received the news that her fiancé had died from wounds received in battle. Some students of her work believe that she modeled Ashley Wilkes in *Gone with the Wind* after Henry. Maybelle Mitchell died three weeks after Christmas in 1919 of the Spanish influenza she caught from nursing other influenza patients. Margaret's own case of the flu delayed her trip home, and she arrived the day after her mother's death. Knowing she was dying, Mrs. Mitchell had dictated a long letter to Margaret through Stephens, Margaret's older brother, specifically saying she must not feel the need to take care of her father.

After her mother's death, Peggy rebelled once again by rejecting her mother's religion and no longer attending church. She completed that year of college but did not return, thus also defying her mother's command to get an education. Instead, she went back to Georgia to do what her mother had forbidden—take care of her father.

Peggy's maternal grandmother moved into the home on Peachtree Street, believing that a young woman should not live alone with men. Peggy's father was hard to please, and Peggy had many conflicts with her grandmother. In fact, after one incident, Peggy's grandmother moved out and led the rest of the Stephens side of the family to cut off contact with Peggy.

Peggy did carry out one of her mother's wishes: She made her debut in society that fall. At the last event of the social season, however, she danced an Apache dance with a Georgia Tech student, which many considered scandalous.

After the social season ended, Peggy started her year as a probationary member of the Junior League, an organization of women volunteers, doing charitable work in a hospital's black and charity wards. In the spring of 1922, the League rejected Peggy's application for membership, partly because of the Apache dance and partly because of her work with the lower class. Peggy never forgot that slight; she refused the reception the League gave in her honor at the time of the 1939 premiere of the movie based on her book.

During the summer of 1919, Peggy underwent an appendectomy. From that time until her death, Peggy experienced frequent sicknesses, disease, accidents, and pain. That winter, she again had a six-week flu. The next summer she displaced her hip and broke her foot. In the fall of 1920, her horse fell with her, injuring her foot again and causing damage to her intestines. She later broke ribs twice. She suffered from chronic insomnia and had bouts of depression throughout her life.

Just past her nineteenth birthday, after observing that a physical illness followed emotional distress that had resulted in depression, she confided to a friend, "I'm as acutely unhappy as it is humanly possible to be and remain sane." Peggy said later that the period from 1919–1922 was the unhappiest time of her life. Yet she continued to write, often at night when she couldn't sleep.

Peggy hid her private unhappiness from the public, however, and by 1922, news of Peggy's charm had spread around Atlanta. She carried only one hundred pounds on her four-foot, eleven-inch frame, yet she had a good figure, auburn hair, and beautiful eyes. Gossip columnist Polly Peachtree wrote: ". . . she has in her brief life, perhaps, had more men really, truly 'dead in love' with her . . . than almost any other girl in Atlanta. For she is a beauty. Then, too, she has a . . . wit." In postwar 1919 Atlanta, Peggy accepted proposals from three men all at the same time without intending to marry any of them.

In the summer of 1922, at age twenty-one, Peggy was dating two men who were roommates, John Marsh and Berrien "Red" Upshaw. To the surprise of her friends, she married Upshaw in September. Red had flunked out of two schools and held only odd jobs, earning a limited living bootlegging whiskey. He had a dull personality and was an alcoholic. The couple lived with Peggy's father and brother, and Red disappeared after two months. Peggy later said that he beat her.

That fall Peggy horrified her father by starting to write for the *Atlanta Journal Sunday Magazine*, earning twenty-five dollars a week. The South had a bias against working women, yet Peggy was achieving her ambition to write professionally. She had to bring in her own hacksaw to cut off the legs of the kitchen chair she was given to sit on because it was too tall for her. Even though she had never studied writing, she surprised her editor and the other writers with the quality of her work and her diligence. Because of her witty personality, people tended not to take her seriously most of the time, and yet she became the first woman to cover hard news for the paper. Her editor praised her work, but she never thought it was good. She showed gumption in her work, such as when she was tied into a boatswain's chair and suspended from a sixth-floor window to share the sensations of the sculptor who had carved a head on nearby Stone Mountain.

Peggy divorced Red in 1924. Divorce was unknown in her family, and that action further alienated her from them.

She then married John Marsh, her copy editor, on July 4, 1925. John helped her immeasurably during her first year on the newspaper staff. Although most of Peggy's friends thought John Marsh was dull and passive, he was well educated, well spoken, and loved literature. He adored Peggy and took her seriously as a writer and as a person in a way no one else ever had before.

They moved into a tiny, dark apartment she nicknamed "The Dump," quite a change from the grand home where she had lived since age twelve. She and John had a very satisfying marriage.

Throughout the 1920s Peggy's illnesses continued. Nine months after her marriage, she developed a chronic arthritic condition that settled in her ankle. She could hardly walk and needed to use heavy orthopedic shoes or crutches. She had to give up her work, so she spent most of her time reading. Each evening John would lug home books from the public library and take them back each morning.

Peggy had been working on two novels, and John encouraged her to write a new novel set in the Old South. He gave her an advance birthday present: a stack of paper, a typing table, and a secondhand typewriter, saying, "Madam, I greet you on the beginning of a great new career." She would write all day, and John would edit the material each night. She kept the effort secret from friends, throwing a towel over her typewriter when they came over.

She wrote the last chapter of her new manuscript first. By 1929, she had written all but the first chapter. She rewrote some chapters as many as twenty times and stuffed them into manila envelopes that filled the tiny apartment. She wrote in the midst of constant personal pain.

In 1932 Peggy and John moved into a larger apartment. Whether true or not, Peggy told friends that she considered tossing

COURTESY OF THE ATLANTA HISTORY CENTER

Margaret Mitchell

out her manuscript rather than going to the trouble of moving it.

In November 1934 a drunk driver plowed into the back of the Marshes' car when both Peggy and John were in it. Peggy's spinal column was fractured, producing long-term nausea and renewed pain in her feet and legs. One doctor put her into a back brace.

In April 1935 John Latham, an editor from the Macmillan Company in New York, stopped in Atlanta on a nationwide trip looking for fresh manuscripts. Lois Cole, Peggy's old friend, worked in the Macmillan office and had heard that Peggy was writing a book. She urged Latham to get in touch with Peggy. "If she can write the way she talks, it should be a honey of a book," Lois said.

When she was first asked, Peggy denied having a novel, but later, she scurried around her apartment, gathering up all but a couple of the chapters. When Latham met Peggy in an Atlanta hotel lobby, he saw a tiny woman seated between two towering stacks of almost seventy dirty brown envelopes that nearly reached her shoulders. "Take the damn thing before I change my mind," she said before she left. Latham started reading the manuscript on the train as he left Atlanta. He knew the book was very good and told his bosses, "We shall make a serious mistake if we do not immediately take it." Peggy couldn't believe that her work was good, and later she wrote Latham, ". . . could I have my manuscript back, please?" Instead, Macmillan gave her a contract. Peggy dedicated the book simply to J. R. M.: John Robert Marsh.

Peggy then began the laborious period of rewriting the book. She agreed to make any changes the editors desired, except to make a happy ending. Further research into the Reconstruction period revealed that much of what she had written was inaccurate. She referred to the revisions as "wholesale butchery, severed arteries, and endless bleeding."

Lifting heavy reference books and sitting for long hours at the typewriter gave her severe back pain. Conflicts arose with the publisher, and Peggy's body, as usual, reacted to her stress. She had a second automobile accident, boils broke out on her scalp, and painful calluses developed on her fingers from all the typing. The calluses had to be removed surgically. During the final weeks of revision, she became bedridden with pain.

Gone With the Wind was formally released on June 30, 1936. Peggy had found the title of the book in the poem "Cynara" by Ernest Dawson, one of her favorite poets. At the front of each stanza was this line: "I forgot much Cynara, Gone With the Wind!" The full title of the poem is "Non Sum Qualis Eram Bonae Sub Regno Cynarae." Peggy had written about a life and a time that was truly gone. The book carried her given name, Margaret Mitchell.

Some students of her work believe that Peggy based the Scarlett O'Hara character on her grandmother, Annie Stephens. Family stories recounted numerous examples of her explosive temper and iron will, and one writer referred to Annie as "a hellion from birth." Both Annie and Scarlett were headstrong women who loved material possessions and bullied others into getting them what they wanted. In addition, both had natural business skills and loved owning property.

In May 1937 *Gone with the Wind* won the Pulitzer Prize, and Peggy instantly became famous. Considered the finest Civil War novel ever written, it remained on bestseller lists longer than any other book in history. Printed in foreign languages around the world, it has outsold all other books ever published, except the Bible.

The book's phenomenal popularity has been ascribed to several factors. First, it dealt with the South and Reconstruction in an original way. Peggy wrote about that period from women's points of view rather than from a military angle. Second, Americans were going through similar experiences in 1936; they had endured a war and were still undergoing the effects of the Depression. The dispirited readers relished reading about people who survived devastating circumstances. The book gave them hope about their own survival.

Sociological explanations aside, Peggy told a very good story. She kept the reader's interest for 1,037 pages, with hundreds of characters and countless incidents. Finally, she wrote a romance that intrigued readers—even beyond the end of the book.

Peggy was not prepared for how fame would affect her life. She and John changed their lifestyle little. She received thousands of letters from fans, and with help from secretaries, she spent three-fourths of her time answering them.

Strangers rang her doorbell, called her on the telephone, and wrote asking for money. They followed her on the street, asking,

"Does Scarlett get Rhett back?" During the casting of the movie based on the book, people even camped outside her apartment, begging her to give them parts. She wrote a friend: ". . . recently as I was leaving the funeral of a cousin, a strange woman had the gall to stop me . . . and ask me to autograph her book. Some people ain't got no notions of decency!"

Resolving contract negotiations exhausted Peggy to such an extent that she awakened one morning blind from bursting blood vessels in her eyes. Bed rest in a dark room restored her vision. In August 1936, John wrote his sister: "Did I tell you that I already have a title for Peggy's next book—the story of the young couple who sowed a 'Gone With the Wind' and were 'Reaping the Whirlwind.'"

Whether she meant it seriously or not, Peggy said, "I hope I'll never write another book. I'd rather scrub floors or pick cotton." And she never did.

David O. Selznick bought the movie rights for $50,000, the highest amount ever paid to that date for such rights. He released the film based on the book in 1939; the premiere took place in Atlanta on December 15, 1939. That day, while attending a luncheon, Peggy missed a chair and fell on the floor. She injured her spine yet again. The stars of the movie attended the premiere, and Peggy and her husband sat with Clark Gable. She was in severe pain during the entire event.

Even though plagued by ill health, Peggy imitated her mother in doing charitable work. In light of her illnesses and the burdens brought about by the book's publication, the movie's appearance, and her sick father, it is amazing that Peggy accomplished as much as she did. While working full time, John assisted Peggy in taking care of *Gone With the Wind* business. Several foreign publishers pirated the work, and the couple spent years trying to get contracts and royalties from those companies. John would sometimes stay up until four o'clock in the morning tending to his wife's business affairs; as a result, he also suffered health problems.

When Germany attacked Britain in the spring of 1940, Peggy plunged into activities supporting in the war effort. She wore a Red Cross uniform and performed a variety of services. She made speeches, and she sold more war bonds and savings stamps than anyone else in Georgia.

When the United States declared war in December 1941, Peggy dove even deeper into defense activities. On September 6, 1941, she christened a new carrier, the USS *Atlanta*. When the Japanese sank it later, she led the Red Cross in a campaign to raise $35 million in bonds to replace the ship. In addition the city raised $65 million, also funding two destroyers. She worked on the Prisoner of War Committee, helping servicemen held captive by the Japanese and Germans.

Peggy gave personal attention to individual servicemen she met in Atlanta, often taking them home with her and feeding them home-cooked Southern meals, and she wrote to hundreds. After the war, she sent relief packages to Europe.

She developed new health problems while nursing her aging father and her husband. She had surgery in January 1940 on abdominal adhesions caused by her appendectomy and first car accident. Her stomach pains did not lessen. Strange symptoms appeared: fevers, diarrhea, fatigue, aching muscles, and headaches.

Finally, in the fall of 1942, Peggy entered the research hospital at Johns Hopkins University in hopes that doctors could find the causes of her illnesses. The physicians could not find any organic cause for her complaints, but a surgeon operated on a ruptured disc. It seemed to Peggy that her surgeon considered her ailments imaginary, which infuriated her. The surgery did not relieve her back pain; instead, she had pain in even more areas of her body.

During Peggy's final twenty years, she was in constant pain. She used back braces, footstools, and cushions to help relieve her discomfort. She could neither sit nor stand with any ease. She had to curtail her volunteer activities, which distressed her.

During these years, John's health problems continued to worry Peggy tremendously. In 1937 he underwent surgery for removal of his gallbladder. On Christmas Eve, 1945, he had a massive heart attack; and in August 1947, he had a second heart attack and had to quit his job. Peggy's father hung near death for eight years, and Peggy visited him twice a day. He died in June 1944.

Despite all of this, Peggy continued helping others in extraordinary ways. She nursed her sick housekeeper and the housekeeper's daughter and visited her laundry woman in the hospital. Her concerns extended beyond people she knew. She funded an annual writing contest among the inmates at the Federal Penitentiary in Atlanta and wrote letters to them. She volunteered at the Florence Crittendon Home for unmarried mothers, giving encouragement and money for them to have permanents and new clothes when they went job hunting.

She funded scholarships for fifty African-American medical students at Morehouse College of Medicine. In their book *Benjamin E. Mays and Margaret Mitchell: A Unique Legacy in Medicine*, Ira Joe Johnson and William G. Pickens suggest that Dr. Mays and Peggy ran "a type of Medical Underground Railroad" where they exchanged letters secretly through their drivers.

> In a real sense, what Mays and Mitchell did was revolutionary. They saw a critical need: no certified black doctors in the state of Georgia and no accredited hospital where blacks could get medical treatment. Mitchell and Mays gave us the Hughes Spalding Hospital [a pay, rather than charity] hospital for blacks and Dr. Otis

Smith, the first black pediatrician in Georgia. Young Morehouse men with aspirations of becoming doctors were allowed to realize their dreams thanks to the largess, vision and humanity of these two individuals.

On August 11, 1949, John and Peggy set out to see a movie. While crossing a street, Peggy was struck by an off-duty, drunk taxi driver as he turned the corner at a high speed. Her skull was fractured, and she died August 16. Her body lies in Atlanta's historic Oakland Cemetery.

The Margaret Mitchell House, Inc., was founded in 1985 to save and preserve the apartment house where Margaret Mitchell lived and wrote the book *Gone with the Wind.* That house (originally a single-family dwelling converted into ten apartments) is one of only four antebellum mansions left on Peachtree Street in Atlanta. The organization oversees the operation of the house, a movie museum, a visitor center, and a museum shop as a permanent landmark, literary center, and tourist attraction. Among other items, visitors can see the typewriter on which Margaret Mitchell wrote *Gone With the Wind* in the restored Apartment #1, "The Dump."

BIBLIOGRAPHY

GENERAL REFERENCES

Fradin, Dennis Brindell. *The Georgia Colony.* Chicago: Children's Press, 1990.

Stevens, William Bacon. *A History of Georgia.* Vol. 1. Savannah, Ga.: Beehive Press, 1972.

Temple, Sarah B. Gober, and Kenneth Coleman. *Georgia Journeys.* Athens: University of Georgia Press, 1961.

White, Reverend George. *Historical Collections of Georgia.* New York: Pudney and Russell, Publishers, 1855.

Willis, Charles A. *Historical Album of Georgia.* Brookfield, Ct.: The Millbrook Press, 1996.

MARY MUSGROVE BOSOMWORTH

Coulter, E. Merton. "Mary Musgrove, Queen of the Creeks: a Chapter of Early Georgia Troubles." *Georgia Historical Quarterly* 11 (1927): 1–30.

Helsley, Alexia Jones. *Unsung Heroines of the Carolina Frontier.* South Carolina Department of Archives and History, 1997.

Johnson, Amanda. *Georgia as Colony and State.* Atlanta: Cherokee Publishing Company, 1970.

Kerber, Linda K. *Women of the Republic: Intellect and Ideology in Revolutionary America.* Chapel Hill: University of North Carolina Press for the Institute of Early American History and Culture, 1980.

Lane, Mills, ed. *General Oglethorpe's Georgia: Colonial Letters 1733–1743,* Vols. 1 and 2. Savannah: Beehive Press, 1975.

Spalding, Phinizy. *Oglethorpe in America.* Chicago: University of Chicago Press, 1977.

SARAH FREEMAN CLARKE

Alcott, Louisa May. *The Journals of Louisa May Alcott.* Edited by Joel Myerson and Daniel Shealy. Boston: Little, Brown, 1989.

"Catalogue of the Clarke Library, Marietta, Ga." Atlanta: Franklin Printing Co., 1896. Original copy in Georgia Room, Cobb County Public Library System, Marietta, Ga.

Cortelyou, P. R. "Address given 26 October, 1893 at opening of Clarke Library, Marietta Ga." Georgia Room, Cobb County Public Library System, Marietta, Ga.

Kopp, Joan Alice, *Sarah Freeman Clarke, 1808–1896: A Woman of the Nineteenth Century.* Marietta, Ga.: Cobb Landmarks & Historical Society, Inc., 1993.

Temple, Sarah Blackwell Glover. *The First Hundred Years: A Short History of Cobb County in Georgia.* Atlanta: Cherokee Publishing Company, 1935.

ELLEN CRAFT

Blackett, Richard J. M. "Ellen Craft." *Black Women in America: An Historical Encyclopedia.* Vol. 1. Brooklyn, N.Y.: Carlson Publishing, Inc., 1993.

Chittenden, Elizabeth F. *Profiles in Black and White: Stories of Men and Women Who Fought Against Slavery.* New York: Charles Scribner's and Sons, 1973.

Craft, William. *Running a Thousand Miles for Freedom: or, The Escape of William and Ellen Craft from Slavery.* 1860. Reprint, North Stratford, N.H.: Ayer Company Publishers, Inc., 1991.

Freedman, Florence B. *Two Tickets to Freedom: The True Story of Ellen and William Craft, Fugitive Slaves.* New York: Peter Bedrick Books, 1971.

Sterling, Dorothy, ed. *We Are Your Sisters: Black Women in the Nineteenth Century.* New York: W.W. Norton & Company, 1984.

REBECCA LATIMER FELTON

Chamberlin, Hope. *A Minority of Members: Women in the U.S. Congress.* New York: Praeger Publishers, 1973.

Felton, Rebecca Latimer. *Country Life in Georgia: In the Days of My Youth.* 1919. Reprint, New York: Arno Press, 1980.

Felton, Mrs. William H. *My Memoirs of Georgia Politics.* Atlanta: The Index Printing Company, Printers and Binders, 1911.

Talmadge, John E. *Rebecca Latimer Felton: Nine Stormy Decades.* Athens: University of Georgia Press, 1960.

Thornton, Richard. "William & Rebecca Felton: The dynamic duo of political reform." *Cartersville Magazine* 1, no. 6 (November-December 1998): 26–32.

MARY ELLEN "NELLIE" PETERS BLACK

Black, Nellie Peters, compiler. *Richard Peters: His Ancestors and Descendants.* Atlanta: Foote and Davies Co., 1904.

Peacock, Jane Bonner. "Nellie Peters Black: Turn of the Century 'Mover and Shaker,'" *The Atlanta Historical Journal* 23, no. 4 (Winter 1979/80): 7–16.

Rucker, Nita Black. Notes. Nellie P. Black Collection, University of Georgia Libraries, Athens.

Shingleton, Royce. *Richard Peters: Champion of the New South.* Macon, Ga.: Mercer University Press, 1985.

JULIETTE GORDON LOW

Behrens, June. *Daisy Low: Founder of the Girl Scouts of America.* Chicago: Childrens Press, 1988.

Brown, Fern G. *Daisy and the Girl Scouts.* Morton Grove, Ill.: Albert Whitman & Company, 1996.

Kudlinski, Kathleen V. *Daisy Gordon Low: America's First Girl Scout.* New York: Viking Kestrel, 1988.

Redford, Ruby L. *Juliette Low: Girl Scout Founder.* Champaign, Ill.: Garrard Publishing Company, 1965.

Shultz, Denny and Daisy Gordon Lawrence. *Lady from Savannah.* New York: Girl Scouts of the U.S.A., 1988.

MARTHA McCHESNEY BERRY

Blackburn, Joyce. Martha Berry: *Little Woman with a Big Dream.* New York: J. B. Lippincott Company, 1968.

Byers, Tracy. *Martha Berry: The Sunday Lady of Possum Trot.* New York: G. P. Putnam's Sons, 1932.

Kane, Harnett T., with Inez Henry. *Miracle in the Mountains.* New York: Doubleday & Co., 1956.

Myers, Elisabeth P. *Angel of Appalachia: Martha Berry.* New York: Julian Messner, 1968.

LUGENIA BURNS HOPE

Beard, Annie. "Mrs. John Hope: Black Community Builder in Atlanta, Georgia, 1900–1936." Masters thesis, Atlanta University, 1975.

Hope, John and Lugenia Burns. Papers. Woodruff Library, Atlanta University Center.

Neighborhood Union Collection. Woodruff Library, Atlanta University Center.

Rouse, Jacqueline A. "Lugenia D. Burns Hope." *Dictionary of Georgia Biography.* Vol. 1. Athens, Ga.: University of Georgia Press, 1983.

————. *Lugenia Burns Hope: Black Southern Reformer.* Athens: University of Georgia Press, 1989.

Shivery, Louie D. "Social Work Among Atlanta Negroes." Masters thesis, Atlanta University, 1936.

Torrence, Ridgely. *The Story of John Hope.* New York: Macmillan Co., 1948.

LEILA ROSS WILBURN

Hunter, Susan. "Lady of the House: Leila Ross Wilburn, Architect." *Southern Homes* (March/April 1989): 136–40.

————. "Women Architects in Atlanta, 1895–1979." *The Atlanta Historical Journal* 23, no. 4 (Winter 1979–80): 85–108.

Ramsey, David. "The Architecture of Leila Ross Wilburn: An Investigation into the Plan Book Process and Ideology in Atlanta from 1910–1940." Ph.D. diss., Georgia Institute of Technology, 1986.

Smith, Susan Hunter. *Atlanta's Lasting Landmarks.* Atlanta: Atlanta Urban Design Commission, 1987.

Wilburn, Leila Ross. *Brick and Colonial Homes: a collection of the latest designs, featuring the most modern in domestic architecture.* Atlanta: Wilburn, 1920.

GERTRUDE "MA" RAINEY

Albertson, Chris. *Bessie.* New York: Stein and Day, 1972.

Harley, Sharon, and Rosalyn Terborg-Penn. *The Afro-American Woman: Struggles and Images.* Baltimore: Black Classic Press, 1978.

Lieb, Sandra. *Mother of the Blues: A Study of Ma Rainey.* Amherst, Mass.: University of Massachusetts Press, 1981.

Oliver, Paul. *The Story of the Blues.* London: Chilton Book Company, 1969.

Smith, Jessie Carney, ed. "Rainey, Gertrude." *Notable Black American Women.* Detroit: Gale Research, Inc., 1992.

Southern, Eileen. *The Music of Black Americans: A History.* New York: W. W. Norton & Co., 1971.

Stewart-Baxter, Derrick. *Ma Rainey and the Classic Blues Singers.* New York: Stein and Day, 1970.

Sullivan, Tom. "Remember Ma Rainey (1886–1939)." Online: www.lambda.net/~maximum/rainey.html (2001).

LILLIAN SMITH

Blackwell, Louise and Frances Clay. *Lillian Smith.* New York: Twayne Publishers, Inc., 1971.

Brewer, Pat Bryan. *Lillian Smith: Thorn in the Flesh of Crackerdom.* Ann Arbor, Mich.: University Microfilm International, 1982.

Cliff, Michelle, ed. *The Winner Names the Age: A Collection of Writings by Lillian Smith.* New York: Norton, 1978.

Gladney, Margaret Rose, ed. *How Am I To Be Heard? Letters of Lillian Smith.* Chapel Hill: University of North Carolina Press, 1993.

Loveland, Anne C. *Lillian Smith: A Southerner Confronting the South.* Baton Rouge: Louisiana State University Press, 1986.

Miller, Kathleen Atkinson. "Out of the Chrysalis: Lillian Smith and the Transformation of the South." Ph.D. diss., Emory University, 1984.

Palumbo, Kathryn. "Summers of Yesteryear at Laurel Falls Camp." *North Georgia Journal* 18 (Autumn 2001): 8–13.

Smith, Lillian Eugenia. *Strange Fruit.* New York: Reynal & Hitchcock, 1944.

————. *Killers of the Dream.* New York: W. W. Norton & Co., Inc., 1949.

————. *The Journey.* Cleveland: The World Publishing Co., 1954.

————. *Now Is the Time.* New York: The Viking Press, 1955.

————. *One Hour.* New York: Harcourt, Brace & World, Inc., 1959.

————. *Memory of a Large Christmas.* New York: W. W. Norton & Co., Inc., 1962.

————. *Our Faces, Our Words.* N.Y.: W.W. Norton & Co., Inc., 1964.

White, Helen, and Redding S. Sugg, Jr. *From the Mountain.* Memphis: Memphis State University Press, 1972.

LEILA DAUGHTRY DENMARK

Bowman, Madia. *Dr. Denmark Said It!* Cumming, Ga.: Caring For Kids, Inc., 1998.

Daughtry-Denmark, Leila. *Every Child Should Have a Chance.* Atlanta: Walsworth/W. H. Wolfe Associates, 1971.

Denmark, Leila. Interview by author. 18 July 2001.

Hutcherson, Mary (daughter of Dr. Leila Denmark). Interviews by author. 22 and 25 July 2001.

May, Lee. "Gardening keeps you young: Pediatrician Leila Denmark's nurturing touch has worked wonders for generations of growing things." *Atlanta Journal Constitution,* 18 July 1994.

McCafferty, Dennis. "The doctor for all ages." *Atlanta Journal Constitution,* 18 April 1992.

Saunders, Tinah. "A life not measured by years: Woman who's oldest working U.S. doctor refuses to be defined by age, popular opinion." *Atlanta Journal Constitution,* 16 March 2000.

Wilkinson, Jack. "There's nothing forgotten in office of Dr. Denmark," *The Atlanta Journal,* 1 April 1986.

MARGARET MITCHELL

Allen, Patrick, ed. *Margaret Mitchell, Reporter.* Athens, Ga.: Hill Street Press, 2000.

Edwards, Anne. *Road to Tara: The Life of Margaret Mitchell.* New York: Dell Publishing Co., Inc., 1983.

Gwin, Yolande. *I Remember Margaret Mitchell.* Lakemont, Ga.: Copple House Books, Inc., 1987.

Harwell, Richard, ed. *Margaret Mitchell's Gone With the Wind Letters 1936–1949.* New York: Macmillan Publishing Co., Inc., 1976.

Johnson, Ira Joe, and Dr. William G. Pickens. *Benjamin E. Mays and Margaret Mitchell: A Unique Legacy in Medicine.* Atlanta: Fourth G. Publishers, Inc., 1996.

Pryon, Darden Asbury. *Southern Daughter: The Life of Margaret Mitchell.* New York: Oxford University Press, 1991.

Walker, Marianne. *The Love Story Behind Gone With the Wind.* Atlanta: Peachtree Publishers, Ltd., 1993.

INDEX

About the Author

Sara Hines Martin is a freelance writer living in suburban Atlanta. She grew up in Virginia and has lived in several states and in two third-world countries. Sara settled in Georgia twenty years ago and has gotten to know her adopted state in the same way she got to know the foreign countries in which she lived: exploring its geography, reading its history, and visiting its sites of interest.

She loves history and has been writing articles and books for forty-five years and now writes for several Georgia magazines and some national magazines for seniors. Her favorite recreation is walking, and in 2001 she published the FalconGuide *Walking Atlanta* with The Globe Pequot Press.